P9-ASM-100

Old Rangoon

Old Rangoon

CITY OF THE SHWEDAGON

by *Noel F. Singer*

Paul Strachan KISCADALE

Published in 1995 by Paul Strachan - Kiscadale Publications
Gartmore, Stirling, FK8 3RJ, Scotland

ISBN 1870838 47 5

Text © Noel. F Singer
Colour photographs © Paul Strachan

All other illustrative materials are from the private collection of Noel F. Singer
with the exception of the following:
on pages 55, 120, 169, 174, 189, 198 by courtesy of the Trustees of the British Library
on page 98 (from the 'Album of William Strang Steel'), 10, 21, 25, 98
kindly loaned by Patricia Herbert

Designed at Kiscadale
Printed in Italy by Milanostampa

Friontispiece: Monastery on the Bahan Road by Paul Strachan

CONTENTS

ရွှေဂုံသူ ရွှေဂုံသားများအတွက်

This book is dedicated to the people of Rangoon (Yangon)

PREFACE

In preparing the text for this work it has not been possible to keep the historical chronology strictly within the geographical confines of Rangoon, which since 1989 has reverted to its previous name Yangon. This is partly due to the fact that changes in the fortunes of those who ruled at Inn Wa (Ava), Toungoo, Pegu, and for a brief period at Syriam, were to have either a fortunate or a detrimental effect on the people who lived in close proximity to the Shwedagon Pagoda.

Rangoon never enjoyed the prestige of being a major administrative centre until its seizure by the British in 1852. Nevertheless, because it fell under the shadow of the great shrine, Burmese Buddhists spoke of it, as they did when referring to that other place of pilgrimage - Pagan - with religious awe and affection. By the colonial period, although the name of the town had been anglicized into Rangoon, its Burmese inhabitants were calling themselves Shwegon-thar and Shwegon-thu - sons and daughters of Shwegon, the Golden [Da]gon or, as the great shrine is known today, the Shwedagon.

In researching the early years of Rangoon's history, accounts by early European travellers have been my main source of information, as native chronicles rarely mentioned the town except as part of some Buddhist myth. I have quoted verbatim the descriptions of contemporary European voyagers, thereby allowing the reader a direct 'feel' for the period. This also provides the opportunity of noting the religious and social prejudices which were prevalent among the authors of the day. Although the text includes incidents of atrocities, it has not been my intention to portray any particular race as the villain. My narrative simply reflects the conditions that existed during the periods described.

Grateful thanks must go to Paul Strachan who first suggested the idea for this volume. Paul had noticed during his visit to Burma (now called Myanmar), that many of the splendid old buildings were being pulled down to make way for new multi-storied structures. Although change is inevitable in an eager young nation just emerging from years of self-imposed isolation, it is, nevertheless, a tragedy that a historical, albeit recent and colonial part of the country's heritage has to be demolished. Writing as someone who grew up in Rangoon, and, like Paul, who has many fond memories of its colourful streets, the sense of loss is also keenly felt by me.

When the British razed Rangoon in 1852-53, prior to building a new city, apart from the ruined pagodas there was little worth preserving. On the other hand, the beautiful old houses, tenements and stately edifices which now fall before the demolition teams can, with a little restoration, add immense charm and character to a splendid city.

I would like to thank Terence Blackburn for his many helpful suggestions, and for allowing me to consult his collection of articles from contemporary British newspapers. To Colleen Beresford for kindly reading the manuscript. Grateful thanks go also to Patricia Herbert for her unfailing advice and assistance and the loan of certain photographs, and to Paul Strachan for providing the invaluable photographs of the grand old buildings which are fast disappearing within the city.

Finally, I would like to make it clear that the views held by me on whether the Shwedagon contains the eight hairs of Buddha, or the reliability of the histories of the Rangoon pagodas are mine alone and not necessarily shared by my publishers.

Noel F. Singer
Shwegon-thar-gyi
Bedfordshire 1995

The Shwedagon

FROM EARLIEST TIMES
TILL 1581

In prehistoric times the area in which the city of Rangoon now stands was dominated by the last summit of a range of hills which stretched out into a shallow sea. Over thousands of years the accumulation of the thick silt deposits brought down by the Irrawaddy, Pegu, and the Sittang Rivers produced the vast flat lands of the Delta. When small groups of migrating tribes, possibly negritos, began their search for permanent sites, a spot as favourable as the one on which Rangoon was later built would have been a natural choice. While the land which sloped gently towards the river was ideal for habitation and agriculture, the thickly forested hills would have provided refuge in case of attack. As religious beliefs evolved over the centuries, the highest of these hills would have been seen as the natural residence of a deity.

Although a specific period was not stated, the earliest historical reference to the people who lived in this region appeared in the *Geographia Syntaxis* (c.AD 125), which was compiled by Claudius Ptolemaeus (Ptolemy). In it he claimed that Lower Burma was inhabited by "cannibals and white-skinned, flat nosed, hairy dwarfs."

Furnivall, in his *Notes on the History of Hanthawaddy* was of the opinion that sometime after 180 BC, when the strongly Buddhist Satavahana-Andhra Dynasty was at the height of its power in India, its merchant-adventurers spread eastwards, founding trading posts along the coastal regions of Burma and other South East Asian countries. Being devout Buddhists, they built stupas on suitably high ground in each locality. He stated that one of the settlements in the Delta was known as Utkala Nagara (town of Utkala); this word is the Sanscrit form of Orissa (also called Kalinga, in

Above: The Shwedagon today from the east or Bahan Gate.
Left: A scene on the Shwedagon. By the early 1900s, the base of the terrace became overcrowded, as well-off Burmese vied with one another to build the most dazzling of shrines. In this picture, tranquillity still prevails. Beato c.1890s. ရွှေတိဂုံရင်ပြင်တော်ရှုခင်း

India), implying that these early colonists decided to name the new region after that of their original homeland. The word was later to be corrupted to Okklapa by the Burmese, and was to be remembered in folklore as a kingdom with its capital somewhere near present-day Rangoon. Furnivall added that there was another town nearby called "Trikumbha Nagara, the Town of the Three Hills, comprising the site of the Shwedagon Pagoda". As an indication of their antiquity, many of these sites in Burma still retain their original Sanscrit names, albeit in a corrupt form. He concluded that these colonists from Orissa were responsible for the introduction of Buddhism to the country, long before the arrival of the Mon and the Burmese.

Conversely, Pearn, in his *History of Rangoon* thought that in historical times, Hindu merchant-adventurers would have discovered the conveniently sited riverine villages of the local inhabitants, and used them as staging posts in their expansion eastwards, thus adding them to a string of others already established by them along the coastline of Burma. [Ptolemy was to list these ports, including the only major one in the Delta, which he called Sabara.]

As most of the country consisted of thick jungle, the Hindu settlers probably kept to the safety of their little enclave. They intermarried with the local inhabitants, who were still at a primitive stage, and because of their superior knowledge and intellect, the newcomers were looked up to by the indigenous population. Pearn suggests that as the settlement became better known among the Hindu seafaring communities and its population increased, a Brahmanical shrine would have been erected on the summit of the nearby hill which must have been already considered sacred. It may be assumed that when the region came under the control of the Mon kingdom of Ramannadesa and into the sphere of Buddhism, either the Hindu temple on the hill was replaced by a Buddhist pagoda, or one was built nearby. Since both faiths flourished side by side, the latter assumption may be more correct. Interestingly, on the present pagoda platform, a smaller stupa known as the Naungdawgyi (Elder Brother), is claimed to be older than the Shwedagon. Thought to mark the site where relics rested before being placed in the Shwedagon, within its core there may well lie either the remains of an ancient Buddhist shrine, or a Hindu temple; this pagoda was raised to its present height in 1876 by U Mon Htaw.

However, as reliable contemporary inscriptions have not yet been found, neither the original name nor the early history of the site and pagoda are known. Burmese and Mon accounts of later ages are so inundated with borrowed incidents from classical Indian literature and miraculous happenings, that the rational mind would have no hesitation in consigning them to the realms of pious fantasy. Nevertheless, it should be borne in mind that the texts were written during a naive and simpler age by genuinely devout and pious members of the Buddhist clergy who did not have deception in mind. The faithful, too, would have thought it a sacrilege to question what was being presented by these venerable men. In Burma, this touchingly trusting and unquestioning attitude has survived into modern times, and the majority of Buddhists still believe implicitly in these medieval texts.

Right: One of the large shrines at the summit of the four covered stairways which led to the vast platform of the Shwedagon. The carvings are by the celebrated U Than Yaung (Mister Colour of Iron). In the building frenzy of the 1880s and 1890s, all such wooden structures were pulled down and replaced by ornamented pavilions and brick stupas. Late 1870s.

အရှေ့မုတ် အာရုံခံတန်ဆောင် ၊ ပန်ပုဆရာကြီ ဦးသံရောင်၏လက်ရာ၊ ၁၈၇၀ခုနှစ်နောက်ပိုင်

The earliest lithic reference to the pagoda, and the sacred hill on which it stands, only appeared in 1476, when Ramadhipatiraja (r.1472-92), the Mon king of Pegu, set up the Kalyani Inscriptions in Pali and Mon. In the Pali text, the nearby river-side town where pilgrims landed was referred to as Tigum-pa-nagara. While in the Mon version, it was called Dgun (a shortened form of Tigum); Dgun was to evolve to Lagun, and later Burmanized to Dagon. In the text, although the official Pali title of the pagoda was listed as Kesa-dhatu-chetiya (Pagoda of the Hair Relics), it was known among the Mon as Kyak Lagun, or Pagoda of Lagun Town.

Ramadhipatiraja later erected the Kyak Lagun Inscription at the site, giving a detailed 'history' of the shrine in Burmese, Pali, and Mon. According to Dr Emil Forchhammer, the German archaeologist, who in 1880 discovered the three inscriptions buried near the summit of the hill, the date of this event was in 1485. Although Forchhammer declined to give dates, he stated that the hill was originally called Singuttara [in Mon Tambagutta] as it formed part of a triangle of three hills; the Sanscrit version was Trikumbhanagara, while Tikumbhanagara was its Pali form.

Conversely, Pe Maung Tin, the Burmese historian and philologist, said that it was known as Trihakumba, which was then corrupted in stages to Trikumba, Dagon, and finally to Lagun. The author appears to have based this statement on a late Mon text known as the *Lik Wan Dhat Kyak Lagun* [History of the Kyak Lagun Relics].

The Imperial Gazetteer which quoted old Mon legends, said that after the town had been established in 585 BC - an impossibly early date when writing did not exist in Burma to record these events — "Punnarika, who reigned in Pegu from 746 to 761 AD, refounded the town, and called it Aramana, and it was not till late that it regained its name of Dagon".

Judging by information issued by the present Pagoda Trustees in 1972, it would appear that records for the shrine only began in 1372, with the raising of the height of the stupa from 27 to 60 feet by the Mon king Bana U (r.1348-83). This would imply that the numerous tales connected with the pagoda prior to this date, which originated from Burmese and Mon sources, must be viewed with caution. In particular, a raid by three kings; Tatabong (Duttabaung), a legendary Pyu king of Sri Kshetra, Norathamanjaw or Aniruddhadeva (r.1044-77), and Mancesu (Minsithu or Jeyasura I, r.1113-60), both of Pagan. These rulers are said to have had intentions of depriving the shrine of its relics, but on each occasion were beaten off by supernatural intervention.

Although the Kyak Lagun has yet to yield up ancient statuary or inscriptions which can be dated either by their iconography, or type of script, finds at other pagodas in and around the area indicate religious activity from as early as the fifth century AD. In the late 1930s investigations by Lu Pe Win of the Department of Archaeology uncovered a vaulted structure and carvings of Buddha in laterite at an old Mon site near Tadagalay. Also excavated nearby was an exquisitely cast bronze Buddha in the Gupta style which was dated to the fifth century AD by Lu Pe Win. A votive tablet with a Pali inscription datable to the 10th century gave the name of the temple complex as Nagasena.

A late Burmese account claimed that another old Mon pagoda, the Kyak Day Ap (in Burmese Botataung) had been erected on the river bank by one hundred *bo* (generals) in AD 947. This was supposedly on the orders of a ruler of Okklapa, mentioned above, who wished to commemorate the spot where his son Min Nanda had been cremated; another source said that it was the king of nearby Twante. Needless to say no contemporary or reliable texts of this event are known.

Bronze Buddha excavated in the vicinity of the Nagasena temple, Tadagalay. 15cm high. c. 5th century

A ridged stupa ofsandstone, with cover and container. 39cm high. Kyak Day Ap (Botataung Pagoda)

U Aung Thaw in his *Historical Sites in Burma* stated that the pagoda was two thousand years old, and that it "contained two corporal relics of the Buddha and a sacred hair". He said, without offering any historical dates or evidence, that it was built by a minister to house these relics which had been obtained from the Mon king of Thaton.

During the Second World War, the Kyak Day Ap was destroyed by a Japanese bomb. Fortunately, the contents of the deeply buried relic chamber remained undamaged. Among the finds was a terracotta votive tablet with an image of a seated Buddha. The obverse of the tablet bore the popular Buddhist formula *ye dhamma hetuppabhava* which had been incised in Mon script by hand while the clay was still wet. Although Nai Pan Hla, the Mon historian, claimed in 1958 that the script was datable to the fifth century AD, Gordon Luce, in 1970, was of the opinion that it was either of the seventh or the eighth century.

Also discovered at this site was a sandstone vessel in the shape of a ridged stupa, containing a four and a half inch high figure of a monk with a huge paunch; the figurine had originally been lacquered and gilded. Assuming that this ornamentation had been applied when the image was made, this could indicate that the use of lacquer and gold leaf was already known to the inhabitants of the area at an early date. Other finds included a cone-shaped reliquary of gold foil decorated with four crudely embossed Buddhas, and a collection of what are believed to be relics.

Again, a word of caution is necessary. Many of the old pagodas in Burma have been rebuilt at one time or another, during which the relic chambers are usually opened and their contents rededicated. This being so, it has not yet been established whether the inscribed tablet and the other objects are contemporaneous with the founding of the shrine, or have been added at a later date from another site.

Image of Saccakapari-bajaka, a Jina ascetic of India commonly known in Burma as the 'Fat Monk'.10cm.

Other ancient stupas which have survived on the outskirts of the present-day city have been modernised in the Burmese style, so that the original Mon features have now been destroyed. These structures were constructed of laterite blocks which were then faced with bricks and covered with stucco. Among the three notable pagodas are the Kyak Ka Lo, the Kyak Waing, and the Kyak Ka San, all of which have fortunately retained their original Mon names. The Kyak Ka San is said to contain a tooth, three hairs, and part of the skull of Buddha; the hairs were claimed to have been borne through the air by eight saints all the way from India.

The little town of Lagun in which these pagodas were sited emerged from obscurity only during the fourteenth century, and was first mentioned in texts pertaining to the period as the scene of intrigue and violence. One such work which was compiled during the sixteenth century by a Mon official called Bana Drala, and known as *Rajadhiraj* states that the Princess Mahadevi, a notorious intriguer and voluptuary who was noted for her amours, was given Lagun as fief by her brother Bana U (r.1348-83), and had a palace there. Bana U's son, Bana Nay, later to become famous as Sutasoma Rajadhiraj (r.1383-1420) eloped with his half-sister, Talamyitau, from the *raja-dhani* the royal city of Pegu, and sought refuge at Lagun. He later rebelled against his father, and again fled to the town where he built a stockaded residence "with a moat and towers", and lived "near the Kyak Athok" (now called the Sule Pagoda).

Cone shaped finial of gold foil with four Buddha images. Octagonal silver base. 11cm high.

Mahadevi and one of her young lovers, the husband of Bana Nay's sister, tried to have him assassinated so that they could seize the crown, but failed. According to the Kyak Lagun Inscription of 1485, when Bana Nay became king, he raised the height of the pagoda, and had its surface encased in sheets of copper, which were then gilded. He made his son Bana Kyan, who was to succeed him, the Governor of Lagun.

In later times, those with ambitions for the Hamsa Throne of Pegu, often used the little port as a base from which to launch an attack on the capital. The standard promise used by such a person when praying before the Kyak Lagun, was that he would offer his weight in gold and regild the stupa from top to bottom if his wish was granted.

Records from the fifteenth century described the glittering religious ceremonies on the terraces of the Kyak Lagun, which were organised by the Mon court. The various accounts also mentioned the appointing of craftsmen and attendants, and of the donations of gold, jewels, and paddy lands for the upkeep of this shrine. At the time, the pagoda treasury was one of the richest in the kingdom and rivalled that of the Kyak Mah Tau [in Burmese Shwemawdaw] the royal stupa at Pegu.

The fame and sanctity of the Kyak Lagun grew, and as the number of pilgrims increased, the authorities began to make improvements to the area with intensive construction work upon pagoda hill. The *Slapat Rajawan Datow Smin Ron* [The History of [Mon] Kings], a work of the second half of the eighteenth century by the Mon abbot, Acwo, said that Bana Ram Kuit (r.1423-46) had the hill cut down. The base was then "built up in five stages" [terraces], and the pagoda was rebuilt to its original height of sixty feet, but the king died while building was in progress. Although work was resumed during the reign of Bana Bawor (r.1446-50), the stupa remained unfinished. It was left to his successor, Bana Ken Dau (r.1450-53) to complete the project.

Among the royal benefactors, the dowager queen Bana Thau (r.1453-72) - who is still referred to in Burmese and foreign accounts as Shin Saw Bu, a name which is quite unknown among the Mon - was the most dedicated, and she spent a vast fortune on the upkeep of the shrine. She also raised its height to 130 feet, gilded the surface with her own weight in gold, and crowned it with a costly finial. A ring of stone lanterns was erected around the base of the pagoda, so that at night, the golden stupa glowed and could be seen for miles.

The *History of [Mon] Kings* said that the queen dedicated :

> four white umbrellas, four golden alms bowls, eight golden curry dishes, four golden spoons, four earthenware vessels, and four offerings were made each day. There were twenty-seven men who prepared the lamps each day. There were twenty men as guardians of the pagoda treasury. There were four goldsmith's shops, four orchestras, four drums, eight doorkeepers, four sweepers, and twenty lamp lighters.

Bana Thau also had the surrounding mounds on the summit levelled, paving stones laid, terraces built, fruit trees planted, and deep ravines filled in. The centuries-old footpaths to the summit were also replaced by four cardinal stairways of bricks and stone, and guarded by five hundred armed men.

Bana Thau acted as head of state until she retired from public life in 1457 and handed over the administration of the kingdom to her son-in-law, the future king Ramadhipatiraja. She built

Right: c.1870s, the area surrounding the stupa still retains the groves of fruit trees and old pavilions which were to disappear in a flurry of building activity in the next decade. This was an indication that the Burmese, under foreign rule, were enjoying a higher standard of living and had money to spend on **religious works.** ၁၈၇၀ခုနှစ်လောက်မှ စိန် လန် စိုပြေလှသော မြတ်ဘုရာ ရွှေတိဂုံရင်ပြင်တော်ရှုခင်

CARVING AT SHWE DAGON PAGODA. RANGOON

Left: The Legend of the Shwedagon. A carved screen depicts the story of the two brothers, Tapussa and Bhallika. The pair are shown arriving in their bullock carts and are being guided by a spirit towards the Buddha on the left, who then presents them with eight hairs from his head. In the small central panel is an unrelated scene from the Vidhura Jataka. The work was commissioned by Ko Pho Khaing and Ma Myit of Botataung, Rangoon, in 1888.

၁၈၈၈ခုနှစ်တွင်ထုလုပ်ထာ သောမြတ်ဘုရာ ရွှေတိဂုံသမိုင်

a stockaded palace on the western side of the pagoda at Lagun, and lived there until her death in 1472. Two small pagodas associated with her have survived; one marked her cremation site, while the other is known as the Pagoda of the Gold Reliquary.

Man's need to glorify a shrine by providing it with an ancient history so as to add an aura of mystery appears to be universal. In their versions of the original texts from India, the Mon authors of the period often put words in the mouth of the Buddha, making him identify the place names of classical India with towns and localities in their country. They also transplanted some of the incidents mentioned in the holy texts to various indigenous localities, claiming that these were the sites at which the scenes had been enacted. Such statements, which were supposedly uttered by the Buddha himself, made the stories extremely plausible. As a result, the faithful still point to these tales as proof that the sacred moments of his previous lives did indeed occur in Lower Burma.

Bana Thau's successor appears in Burmese and modern foreign accounts as Dhammaceti, a title which was never used during his reign - in his inscriptions the monarch always referred to himself as Ramadhipatiraja (r.1472-92). The king, who was once a celebrated monk, made extensive repairs to the Kyak Lagun, regilding it regularly, though he never raised its height. In 1476, he donated a huge finely cast bronze bell called Ahwinga Sauk, the surface of which was covered in inscriptions from top to bottom, and was one of the great art treasures of this period; it weighed 3,000 viss (almost five tons).

In 1485, after consultation with the leading ecclesiastics in his kingdom, the king had the history of the pagoda engraved in his Kyak Lagun Inscription. Despite most of its legendary contents, towards the end of the text the historical accounts concerning members of the ruling Wa Row dynasty (1287-1538) are invaluable.

In that part of the text which can only be considered legendary, events in the early Indian Buddhist works such as the *Anguttara Nikaya*, and the *Mahavagga* of the *Vinaya Pitaka* were altered to fit in with Ramadhipatiraja's own line of thinking; this was done no doubt through feelings of extreme piety. The nationality of the two leading characters called Taphussa and Bhallika (in Mon Tapu and Tabaw), were also changed, and they were depicted as natives of the Mon country. Hitherto, information concerning the brothers was lacking in the older texts from

Above: A group of worshippers on the Shwedagon Pagoda. In the background can be seen a *monok-thiha* (sphinx-like monster from Mon mythology) and its *chinthe* (lion) attendants. The sign in front of the sphinx states that this is the Tuesday corner, and people born on that day are expected to use the spot to pray and make offerings. This area at the base of the pagoda is now densely covered with small shrines. ရွှေတိဂုံရင်ပြင် အင်္ဂါထောင့်မှ ဘုရား ဖူး များ

India, the Kyak Lagun Inscription and Mon works of later periods, such as the *Lik Wan Dhat Kyak Lagun*, and the *Slapat Tapphussa-Bhallika*, now provided it in abundance. In the latter, Buddha is even made to reveal the seven ancient names of the sacred hill of the Kyak Lagun. These were: Trihakumba, Sattabhummi, Dhannavati, Pokkharavati, Bhuridatta, Siharaja, and Tambagutta - a confused collection of Sanscrit and Pali names; Bhuridatta being the title of a Jataka (birth story of Buddha), and Dhannavati, a city in Arakan.

According to the Mon history of the Kyak Lagun, the two merchants, Taphussa and Bhallika, travelled from Lower Burma to India, where Buddha presented them with some hairs from his head. Eventually, the relics were brought back to Tambagutta Hill, and after many events involving supernatural beings, were enshrined in a relic chamber knee-deep in gems and guarded by demons. In reality the pair were natives of Orissa, in India, and never left their country of origin.

The people who were later to become known as the Myanmar (Burmans) were still in their original homeland in north-west China, when these incidents allegedly took place twenty-five centuries ago. Though they had yet to begin their long migration into the Irrawaddy valley, some of their later accounts were to claim Taphussa and Bhallika as their own.

Stranger still, in Sri Lanka, the *Mahavamsa* [Chronicle of the Greater Dynasty] a work which spans the fifth to the twelfth centuries, mentions another, the *Kesa Dhatu Vamsa* [History of the Buddha's Hair Relics], which said that the place of enshrinement of the hairs, was at Orissa, in India; no mention was made of Mon merchants or the Kyak Lagun. It added that these relics were finally brought to Sri Lanka in 490 AD and placed in a dagaba (where they have remained to this day).

Rhys Davids, the eminent Pali scholar, describes how "we have here an interesting instance of the growth of legend to authenticate and add glory to local relics. The ancient form of this legend, must have arisen when the relics were still in Orissa. Both the Burmese and the Ceylonese now claim to possess them". The historian, Harvey, was to add that although the legend of the sacred hairs was included in the *Mahavastu*, one of the earliest known Sanscrit works on the life and incidents involving the Buddha, "when first told it had no reference to Burma".

In the fifteenth century, Lankadipa or Sri Lanka was celebrated throughout the Buddhist world for being the repository of the Buddha's hairs, tooth, collar bone, and begging bowl. It could be that the Mon King Ramadhipatiraja wished to attract some of the glory to his kingdom by circulating, and putting on permanent record in the Kyak Lagun Inscription, his version of the story of the hair relics. As the ultimate attraction it was also claimed that enshrined beneath the pagoda were the miraculously preserved water-dipper of Kakusandha, the bathing-garment of Konagamana, and the staff of Kassapa; the three previous Buddhas. This claim was to make the Kyak Lagun the premier site of Buddhist importance outside India.

The *History of [Mon] Kings* states that the collection beneath the pagoda also included the "eyetooth and the Adam's apple of the exalted Ari Mettaya" - the future Buddha who has yet to appear. Therefore, it seems curious that although obscure little shrines all over Burma claim to have been honoured by a visit from Buddha, the Kyak Lagun should have been pointedly omitted by the Holy One.

Ramadhipatiraja's subtle form of religious propaganda, which was possibly done with the best intentions, obviously succeeded, for with an unmatched collection of relics of this magnitude

THE KYAK LAGUN INSCRIPTION

This venerable cetiya of the hair relics of the exalted Buddha enshrined by Tapussa (and) Bhallika on the top of the Tambagutta hill, at the time when His Majesty the Lord of the White Elephant, named Dhammatrailokyana-thaarajadhirat [r.1348-83], was king, the prasada which was the cetiyaghara, having been severed asunder [by earthquake], was encased (and) enlarged (by him and) when encased was 40 cubits high.

Thereafter, at the time when His Majesty Sutasomarajadhirat [r.1383-1420] was king, (he) caused it to be encased (and) enlarged again, and when it had been encased (and) enlarged (he) erected...the spire (and) set up the umbrella (and) putting a layer of copper within (and) putting a layer of gold outside (he) had the whole of the spire fully overlaid.

Thereafter, at the time when His Majesty Ramarajadhirat [r.1423-46] was king, in the year 798 [1436] of the Common Era, the venerable cetiya of the hair relics, (so far as) all that had been raised from the shoulder of the bell upwards (is concerned) having collapsed, His Majesty together with (his) queen Narajadevi ordered Prince Samm Mlam to level... and have (it) built up again. When (it) had been built up again (they) had it plastered. They, saying that the cetiya was very small, from the large plinth (upwards they) had it rebuilt (and) encased once more. The building (and) encasing of the cetiya had not been completed when His Majesty Ramarajadhirat departed to the city of the devas.

Thereafter, at the time when His Majesty Bana Barwor [r.1446-50] styled Jayaddisarajadhirat was king, His Majesty together with (his) queen Ray, having given many offerings, had (it) built up (and) encased.

His Majesty's mother, the Queen Viharadevi, together with Yogarat, the commander-in-chief of the army, exerted themselves: all the slaves, followers (and) retainers that there were (they) led forth to build, but the building had not been completed when His Majesty Jayaddisarajadhirat departed to the city of the devas.

Thereafter, at the time when His Majesty Bana Ken Dau [r.1450-53] styled Dhammatrailokyanatharajadhirat, was king, what His Majesty's mother Queen Viharadevi had built was finished. When it had been finished His Majesty Bana Ken Dau, styled Dhammatrailokyanatha, had it plastered, erected the spire (and) set up the umbrella.

Thereafter, at the time when Her Majesty Sri Tribhuwanadityapravara-dhammatrailokyanatha Mahadhammarajadhirajdevi [Viharadevi or Bana Thau (1453-72)] together with her son named Ramadhipati Sri Paramamahadhammarajadhirat [r.1472?-92)] were rulers, (they made) many offerings together with all the forces of their army. Their Majesties, mother and son, having gone to dwell at the foot of the hair relics, had the hollows (of the ground) filled up, ...arranged stone umbrellas overlaid with gold, and between the umbrellas (they) had the foot of the plinth of the cetiya paved throughout with flat stones, (and) having (on) the foot of the plinth built up the bell, (they) arranged standing lanterns made of stone... **Epigraphia Birmanica.**

The Mon Queen Bana Thau (Shin Saw Bu). Drawing based on terracotta plaques of the period.

Fytch Square with Sule Pagoda and the original Town Hall.

concentrated at the Kyak Lagun, the shrine could not fail to attract pilgrims, who are reported to have been drawn from the "eight directions".

As Buddha's relics were believed to be capable of duplicating themselves, by the fifteenth century, thirty-three shrines scattered across the Mon country alone were each listed as being repositories of the tooth; according to some accounts the number was said to be forty. Not to be outdone, the records of other pagodas insisted that they, too, held a hair which had been presented by Buddha himself; the Arakanese, Burmese, and the Shan have also claimed similar relics.

An example of how a variety of legends can be created by the pious to glorify a particular religious site can also be seen at the Kyak Athok (Sule Pagoda). Modern-day Buddhists now insist that this small shrine is connected with the founding of the Kyak Lagun. They claim that it had been built to mark the spot where the two brothers, Taphussa and Bhallika carrying the hairs landed on their return from India. The pair are said to have begun their search for Tambagutta Hill from this spot.

U Aung Thaw, on the other hand, ignores this version and states that of the ten sacred hairs brought by Sona and Uttara, the Indian missionaries, one was given to Maha Sura, the minister of Lagun, who then enshrined it in a pagoda named after himself. The name of the shrine then evolved from Sura to Sule.

Another variant of the legend was that eight saints from Sri Lanka rested at the spot where the Sule Pagoda was later to be built. They then went in search of a magic ruby which had the power to prevent their island from being eroded by waves. Having found the ruby across the river at Trawn (Syriam), they gratefully gave the minister in charge of Lagun a sacred hair; this was duly enshrined in the Sule Pagoda.

While one source states that the word Athok was the name of the fortunate minister, another claimed that it was an old Mon word meaning "a sacred hair". So far, no historical material has been found to substantiate these claims. Whatever its origins, the earliest historical reference to the pagoda only appeared in the *Rajadhiraj,* mentioned above. In this account it is recorded that, when Bana U (r.1348-83) came on a pilgrimage to the Kyak Lagun during the latter part of his reign, paranormal manifestations were reported at the Kyak Athok. The king acknowledged these miraculous events by holding celebrations at the site for seven days.

By the second half of the fifteenth century, the town of Lagun had acquired a reputation as a religious centre due to the large number of learned monks within its numerous monasteries. It was also famous for the twenty-two ordination halls to which men from all over the kingdom and the surrounding Buddhist countries came to be inducted into the Buddhist priesthood. Ramadhipatiraja decreed that as the people of Lagun lived within the sacred boundary of the shrine, they should refrain from eating meat; an unpopular stipulation which was ignored after his death. He also commanded that the official in charge of Lagun was to make offerings to the pagoda on feast days, in particular at the beginning and the end of the Buddhist Lent; this custom was continued by all the kings of the various dynasties who came after him. At the annual festival in March it was noticed that people arrived in vast numbers, and to cater to their needs a bazaar was organised which quickly grew into a huge trade fair. This tradition, too, was to last well into the 1840s.

Lagun's administrative centre, where the local gentry lived, was protected by a stockade of huge teak logs and sharpened bamboo defences, while on the outside of this barrier were clustered the houses of the common folk. The inhabitants were mainly artisans, fisherfolk, merchants, and descendants of pagoda slaves; the latter served the pilgrims by selling religious artifacts and offerings, and attended to the great pagoda. Other inhabited areas were along the river-bank and the roads leading to the shrine.

Lagun was also a cult centre for spirit worship. The *Nidana-arambhakatha,* a work of the sixteenth century, said that when Ramadhipatiraja made offerings of food, white umbrellas, prayer flags, gold and silver lamps, to the thirty-six dewatau (gods) of his kingdom, he included the five at Lagun. Each spirit shrine was centred around a large tree, usually a banyan (*ficus religiosa*) in which the deity was believed to reside. It had resident mediums and attendants who were there to minister to the worshippers, tell fortunes, sell charms, and organise the annual festival with music and dance.

The account said that the images of the five gods at Lagun were to be found at: the tree in the Grove of the Indian Lady; at the Kyak Athok or Sule Pagoda, where a modern Burmese carving of an entity known as the Sule Nat or spirit can still be seen; the tree at the Mouth of Lagun, situated to the east of the Botataung Pagoda; the Lip of Lagun; and the Hill of Iron, which was the residence of the spirit known as the Iron Master. Unfortunately, only one of these five sites can now be identified. As the banyan tree can live to a great age, these cult centres were already old when the work was written sometime during the sixteenth century.

With the death of Ramadhipatiraja, the power of the Mon kings began its slow decline. In 1492 a terrible cyclone brought destruction to the land, and Lagun appears to have borne the full force. The chronicles claimed that the winds were of such velocity that they ripped the finial off the Kyak Lagun and "it fell down as far away as Syriam" on the opposite bank. It was left to Hatthiraja, or Bana Ram (the Tiger), (r.1492-1526) to restore the Kyak Lagun.

The shrine was to undergo further damage during his long reign, and had to be repaired several times. When the king "reached the age of forty-eight, he built forty-eight little pagodas on the base" surrounding the great stupa; its height was also increased. These were to be the last grandiose works to be carried out under a Mon king. His successor, the sixteen year old Badhiroraja (The Deaf), or Daka Rat Pi, (r.1526-39), could only offer a "chain of gold adorned with sapphires and many different kinds of precious stones" to be put "on the dome of the pagoda".

In 1539, the more aggressive Burmese of the north seized their chance, and led by Tabinshwehti (r.1531-50), annexed Pegu. Overwhelmed by the onslaught, Daka Rat Pi abandoned his capital and fled. As Burmese influence began asserting itself in what was once the old Mon kingdom, many of the Mon names for pagodas and towns began to be Burmanized. Kyak Lagun and its little town came to be known as Dagon. Althought as late as 1649, the posthumous Rajamanisula Pagoda Inscription of Thalun (r.1629-48), in Upper Burma, included the old Mon form of Tigum when referring to the town. In foreign accounts of the sixteenth century the town appears as either Dogoune or Dogon. The *Mahayazawingyi*, or Great Royal Chronicle, which was compiled by U Kala in 1724 and is one of the earliest known Burmese works, refers to the stupa as the Dagon-san-daw-shin or Dagon of the Hair Relics.

The Burmese king, Tabinshwehti, spent much of his reign on the battlefield, sacking with great cruelty Martaban, one of the richest ports in the East; its ruler and most of its inhabitants were massacred. He then turned his attention to Prome and crushed that state with savagery. Shin Thayet, the king who reigned there was only thirteen, and was married to his thirty-six year old aunt. Fernao Mendes Pinto, who was reputedly an eye witness, said that Tabinshwehti had the queen paraded up and down the streets stark naked, and then had her "publicly whipped and delivered up to the lust of the soldiers until she died. The young king was tied to her dead body and cast into the river. The same was done with 300 gentlemen, after stakes were drove through their bodies".

Tabinshwehti finally decided to win over the Mon by more subtle means. Seemingly he cherished the Mon way of life and culture, and to impress his new subjects placed a jewelled finial on the Dagon Pagoda. During the dedication ceremony he even presented his chief queen as an offering, but redeemed her from the terrible fate of a pagoda slave with a large amount of gold bullion. Pinto said that gold reserves were placed for safekeeping in the pagoda, and that he saw a large solid gold Buddha studded with emeralds and rubies, which he considered to be the most valuable object in the world.

In about 1548, the king formed a strong attachment for a disreputable Portuguese youth, the nephew of Diogo Soarez de Mello, the Captain-General of his mercenaries, and under his influence spent his days in drink and dissipation. Taking advantage of the increasing chaos at the Burmese court, some of the Mon lords seized Dagon in 1550 and tried to reassert their independence under Smin Dhaw Juk Lali, another son of Bana Ram, the Tiger. The town was the scene of a fierce battle and the rebellion was put down by the Burmese; Smin Dhaw Juk Lali escaped in the confusion.

Tabinshwehti, who was now incapable of ruling, became increasingly paranoid, and began putting to death innocent people at court. Unable to stand this tyranny, Smin Dot, the Mon lord of Sittaung, lured the king into the jungle and cut off his head; the eyelids of the dead king are said to have twitched for several hours, much to the amazement of the onlookers.

Shwedagon today: devotees make offerings to the Buddha and the symbol of the weekday of their birth

Smin Dot recaptured Dagon from the Burmese, seized Pegu and proclaimed himself king. During his reign of three months he donated a new gold finial studded with gems for the Dagon Pagoda. However, this devotional act which was performed in gratitude for the change in his fortunes, failed to protect him from the bullet of Gonzalo Neto, a Portuguese assassin belonging to the camp of his rival Smin Dhaw Juk Lali. The new king, who assumed the title of Smin Dhaw Rama, was to be the last of the Wa Row dynasty. He reigned for one year, during which he was forced to hand over the traitor, Diogo Soarez de Mello, and uncle of Tabinshwehti's boon companion, to a howling mob who promptly tore him to pieces.

Smin Dhaw Rama was challenged to single combat by Bayinnaung (r.1551-81), the charismatic brother-in-law of Tabinshwehti. The contest was fought during a violent thunderstorm which was said to have suddenly appeared after Bayinnaung had prayed in true heroic fashion, 'As upholder of the Faith may I be the victor'.

Predictably, Smin Dhaw Rama was vanquished and fled with his army. Defiant Pegu paid the price, and almost all its inhabitants were massacred by the Burmese, "not even their animals were spared". When the ex-king was finally captured, he refused to bow down before the Burmese ruler, and as a consequence was beheaded.

During his reign, Bayinnaung, also known as Hanthawaddy Sinphyumyarshin, or Lord of the Many White Elephants of Hanthawaddy, founded an empire which stretched from Manipur to Thailand. While magnificence prevailed at his court, in the countryside there was poverty, and the people were terrorised by bands of marauding bandits, rebels, and slavers. Pegu had to be rebuilt twice, due to enemy action, but was to became one of the richest and most populated cities in the East, as thousands of captives, which included skilled artisans, and treasure from the conquered states, poured in. The Mon, in abject terror, gave Bayinnaung the title of Jamnah Duih Cah (Conqueror of the Ten Directions).

Caspar de Cruz, a Dominican missionary, who was in the country between 1550 and 1560, said that the "Brames" (Burmese) were "a great people, very rich of gold and precious stones, chiefly of rubies; a proud nation, and valiant. They are somewhat like the Chinas (Chinese) in their faces; they have very rich and gallant shippings garnished with gold [gilded boats], in which they sail in the rivers; they use vessels of gold and silver; their houses are of timber and very well wrought. The kingdom is very great".

The empire was to become even greater after the conquest of Ayutthaya by Bayinnaung in 1567. Soon after this event, a Thai named Aukbya Setki, was made Lord of Dagon. He was a traitor who had collaborated with the Burmese king and brought about the destruction of his immensely wealthy city. Despite being given the town of Peikthalauk (Phitsanulok) in Thailand, he prudently remained at Dagon, where he was awarded the property of military chiefs who were executed for their failure to come up to the king's expectations.

In 1572, Bayinnaung raised the height of the Dagon Pagoda to 300 feet and had it regilded. The shrine had been reduced to rubble during a violent earthquake in 1564. Mon accounts which give the date of this terrifying event as 1568, said that a total eclipse had preceeded the earthquake, and that "day was like night" and people thought that the end of the world had arrived. Like the kings of old, Bayinnaung used the jewels from his crown and other regalia, to adorn the *hti* (cone-shaped finial). He also dedicated 500 pagoda slaves.

The *Mahayazawingyi* stated that when another earthquake caused the finial of the Dagon Pagoda to fall in 1573, the king came on a second pilgrimage. He rode in a huge golden barge, the figurehead of which was shaped like that of a *hamsa* (sacred goose and emblem of the Mon); the rest of the court were in their own barges each of which had a different figurehead. The royal progress was protected by 300 *hlaw-gar* (large golden canoes), and 1000 *taik-hle* (war boats). A second finial, set with gems from another crown was installed, and tinkling bells of solid gold, silver, and other metals were donated by the court. During the celebrations which followed immense pyramids of oil lamps were lit for five nights.

Bayinnaung's last progress to the Dagon Pagoda was in 1581, when the same flotilla of gilded vessels appeared on the Pegu River. The chronicle said that the great mass of boats covered the surface of the water as far as the eye could see and filled the air with a cacophony of musical sounds.

The king died a few months later in Pegu of what is suspected to have been a massive heart attack. It was reported that "on that day the great pagoda [Mahaceti, which housed a fake tooth of Buddha from Sri Lanka] fell into ruins [collapsed], and an inundation covered the whole city [of Pegu]".

Right: The approach to the Shwedagon across the platform from the East or Bahan entrance.

မြန်မာပြည်နှင့်ကုလားဖြူများ
Kala-Phyu

WHITE FOREIGNERS
IN LOWER BURMA
1583-1800

Although European travellers began visiting the country from the early 1430s, the first account of Dagon was provided only in 1583 by the Venetian, Gasparo Balbi. He said that the landing place at Dagon had a broad flight of wooden steps which were guarded by a pair of huge wooden tigers "with open mouths showing their teeth and tongue, with their claws uplifted and stretched forth, preparing to assail him that looks on them" he added that they were "painted after the natural colour of the Tiger". There were two more of these beasts further up the stairs. The local belief was that the tigers would come to life and attack all who had evil intentions on the treasures of the shrine. Most scholars insist that Balbi was confusing the *chinthe*, or sacred Burmese lion, with a tiger, but since his description is quite clear, there is no reason why it should not have been the latter. Tigers were so numerous in the region that they were to pose a threat to the inhabitants of the town until well into the 1800s; one of the many titles of the Mon rulers was Lord of the Elephant and the Tiger - the Sin Kyar Shin which some of the Burmese kings adopted.

Balbi said that the long avenue [over two miles] which led to the pagoda was fifty paces broad and shaded with trees. While the right hand side of the road was reserved for houses, gilded monasteries, shrines, and gardens, on the left was a continuous row of shops and resting places for travellers.

This Pilgrim's Way terminated at the south entrance of the pagoda and was guarded by a third pair of tigers, but these were of stone. There were ninety steps leading up to the summit and these were divided into three sections. Balbi said that on the last steps were "angels of

Above: the Sule Pagoda today from Independence Park.
Left: A *wungyi* or minister in Procession, from a *parabaik* or folding book. c. late 1820s. ဝန်ရှင်မင်း ကြီး ခမ်း ကြီး နား ကြီး နှင့်ထွက်သည့် ပုံ

A Mon deva, as described by Gasparo Balbi

stone, each with three crowns one above the other...they have the right hand lifted up, ready to give the benediction, with two fingers stretched out". The hill on which the pagoda stood had been reshaped into three terraces with retaining walls, along which were planted fruit trees.

On the summit, the wide platform around the great gilded stupa was encircled by ordination halls and prayer pavilions blazing with gold. Balbi noted that the height of the pagoda was just a little below that of St. Marks' bell-tower in Venice. Other attractions were the numerous religious statuary including stone figures of the six demon-kings which were believed to guard the relic chamber. The Mon abbot, Acwo, said in his *History of the [Mon] Kings* that these ancient statues of the sentinels could still be seen until the second half of the eighteenth century. He lists them as Smin Gaw Chaai, Smin Jambuka, Smin Pok Lha, Smin Sa, Yaksha Punnaka, and Smin Jaiyya. They were led by the awesome Smin Guiw Daai (Glowing Red King). Also on view were a collection of large bronze bells, among which was the magnificent Ahwinga Sauk donated by Ramadhipatiraja in 1476.

The exotic sights certainly impressed Balbi, for he said that it was "the fairest place, as I suppose, that is in the world". Some modern authors were to misinterpret this quote by saying that the Venetian was referring to the town and not to the pagoda. Balbi had arrived on November 2 1583, a few days after a Buddhist festival had been celebrated at the full moon, this meant that the town was still crowded, hence his description of the place as the "fair city of Dogon". However, Pearn in his *History of Rangoon* was to correct their error. He added that there was a surge of human activity in the area only during one of the numerous feast days, at the end of which the place reverted back to being a peaceful riverine town.

Whenever important events in the Buddhist calender were held at Dagon, it was a tradition for members of the ruling family and courtiers to come down from Pegu on a flotilla of golden barges. The court camped in strongly fortified temporary enclosures for the duration of the festival, which included entertainments of all kinds. Ralph Fitch, the Elizabethan traveller who claimed to have visited Dagon in 1586, said that at such times, a man could hardly pass by land or water because of the "great presse of people". Many came with their produce to the huge fair which was held on an open plain between the pagoda and the town, and where all types of goods, foreign and local, could be obtained.

In the region, fishing appears to have been a major industry, for Balbi complained that the numerous nets which were set by the fisherfolk were a great danger to vessels. The creeks and rivers around the town were fast flowing, and boats often became entangled and were dragged down into the depths by the strong undercurrents and tidal surges. He also noted that the rivers which flowed by Dagon and "Sirian" (Syriam) were effected by a "Maccareo", a violent tidal bore, which some of the more experienced vessels used to their advantage to ride up part of the way to Pegu; the tidal bore no longer exists in the area.

In the 1580s, traders from abroad were still attracted to the great metropolis and emporium of Pegu where exotic merchandise was available. They have left glowing accounts of the wealth of its king, Ngasudayaka (r.1581-99), the sadistic son of Bayinnaung, and of the rich pickings to be made at the capital because precious stones, such as rubies, were cheap. To reach the city, these travellers had to pass either Dagon, or the nearby port of Syriam, both of which were used as staging posts. The latter was described as a "good town and hath a faire port into the sea whither come many ships from Mecca, Malacca, Sumatra and from divers other places. And there the ships stay and discharge and send up their goods in Paroes (boats) to Pegu".

A Portugese mercenary of the 16th Century.

Despite the prosperity which was to last for a few more years, the imperial days of Pegu were already beginning to wane. This was in part caused by the ruthless policies of the mass murderer, Ngasudayaka, which were ultimately to lead Lower Burma into anarchy. In 1582, during a brief moment of guilt, the king atoned for his evil deeds by donating a richly jewelled finial for the Dagon Pagoda. He built a cordon of forty eight small shrines around the base of the stupa, and offered a large bronze bell. Two enclosure walls were also erected around the hill, and a brick road lined on both sides with a continuous row of eighteen-foot high pagodas was built all the way to the principal landing stage at Dagon.

In 1583, Balbi witnessed the terrible sight of hundreds of grandees and their families being burnt in a huge cage and soon after, the already tense situation at Pegu began to deteriorate. The Venetian narrates that ten days after this event he "saw the King upon an elephant all over covered with gold and jewels go to the war [with Ava] with great courage, with a sword after our custom, sent him by the Viceroy of Goa, the hilt whereof was gilded: the said Viceroy was called Don Louis de Zuida. The two kings met and fought body to body without any hindrance of the armies...as did also the Guard of this king with that of the other, and after the kings had fought a while, hand to hand, first with arquebusses, then with darts [javelins], and lastly with the sword, the elephant of the king of Pegu broke his right tusk with charging that of Ava".

Ngasudayaka won the combat, and instigated a campaign of oppressive measures which resulted in massacres, civil wars, and unrest throughout Lower Burma. This effectively prevent the cultivation of vital food crops so that many died of famine. Added to all these horrors were devastating outbreaks of smallpox which killed thousands. Those who survived were to face another crisis in 1596, as the region was invaded by vast hordes of field rats which devoured all the stored grain, causing a great famine.

Aquatint of the Shwedagon from
Joseph Moore's *Eighteen Views
Taken at or Near Rangoon* (1825-6).

A tidal bore on the
Sittang River.
The Graphic, May 8 1875.

ဒီလှိုင်းလုံးကြီး၏အန္တရာယ်

Nicholas Pimenta, Visitor General of the Jesuits, quoting eyewitness accounts in 1599, reported that as the inhabitants of Pegu starved, they had no choice but to resort to cannibalism. He said that "parents abstained not from their children, and children devoured their parents. The women went about the streets with knives to like butchery purposes".

Possibly, because of a deep sense of shame, the native chronicles are understandably silent about this horrifying episode in Burmese history, only commenting rather mildly, that during the reign of Ngasudayaka the people experienced much misery and sorrow. It should be remembered that many of these chronicles were written for the court, which meant that their authors would not have dared record anything which would have been detrimental to the reputation of the ruling family.

Earlier, Father Pietro Bonfer who was in the country between 1550 and 1557, had likened the inhabitants of Lower Burma to those of Sodom, as they were "addicted to a number of sins, specially of lubricity [lewdness], perpetrating the most villainous and heinous crimes against nature, without the least shame or confusion". A shocked Bonfer had no doubt been told that Burman and Mon alike indulged in the custom of inserting up to three small round bells *(chu)* in their penis. Ralph Fitch was more forthcoming on this somewhat bizzare practice and explained that it had been invented for the men of "Pegu, Ava, Langeiannes [Vientiane], Siam, and the Bramas, so that they should not abuse the male sex, for in times past all those countries were given to that villainy, that they were very scarce of people". Fitch was doubtless referring to homosexual practices which were once more prevalent.

This exotic tradition of wearing "bunches of little round balls in the privy members" was known in other Southeast Asian countries, and was mentioned as early as 1435 by Nicolo di Conti who said that at the Burmese capital of Ava (Inn Wa), old women earned their living by "selling Bels of gold, silver, brass, of the bigness of Nuts, which they put in mens yards betwix the skin and flesh, when they are of age to use Women; and the men much please themselves to hear the sound of them as they goe".

Fitch was to add "they say the women do desire them", and that the incision took up to "eight days" to heal. Other accounts indicate that once used, these little bells which were sometimes gilded, were removed and exchanged among the men of the ruling classes. The practice was noted by Valentyn in Arakan as late as 1724. Harvey, writing in 1924, commented that "one hears vaguely of shot being used in the same way in Indian towns nowadays".

In Lower Burma of the mid sixteenth century, all this 'wickedness' was too much for the celibate Bonfer. The Jesuit was to say that he also "found the hearts of the inhabitants so obstinate that he was unable to obtain" any converts, and that he had no alternative but to leave the country, "shaking the dust off one's feet for a testimony of the stubbornness of the inhabitants, and of the misfortune that shall befall them". He added that he would rather "preach among pigs than among such a swinish generation".

The disparaging comments about the people of Burma which exist in various missionary accounts probably began from this period, and were to reach a peak during the nineteenth century. Frustrated at being unable to 'save' these so-called "barbarous heathens" since they were quite content with Buddhism, these self appointed 'soul-savers' resorted to denigrating their usually generous hosts. Possibly, to Bonfer's immense delight, his dire prediction concerning the state of the country subsequently came true.

In Lower Burma, the 1590s were to culminate in the devastating wars between the Arakanese, Burmese, and the Thai. These were harsh and terrible times, in which those who wished to remain in control had to take excessive measures. Such attitudes and supressions were not confined to Burma alone but were being enacted in other countries of the period.

Burmese Fortunetellers.

Boves, another Jesuit, who was at Syriam in 1600, said that it was "a lamentable spectacle to see the banks of the rivers set with infinite fruit-bearing trees, now overwhelmed with ruins of gilded temples and noble edifices; the ways and fields full of skulls and bones of wretched Peguans [Mon], killed or famished or cast into the river, in such numbers that the multitude of carcases prohibits the ways and passage of any ship".

Ngasudayaka, the king of Pegu, was carried off by the ruler of Toungoo, together with much of the loot of Ayutthaya, and managed to survive until 1603. During his exile, the ex-king made himself so obnoxious that one dark night Prince Natshinnaung, the poet-warrior, bludgeoned him to death while he was in the act of entering the women's apartments. Peter Williamson Floris, the Dutch traveller, said that the murder weapon was a "pilon" (a thick wooden pestle used for pounding rice).

Pegu, that magnificent city, where conquered kings with hatred in their hearts for the Burmese had no option but to bow low before Bayinnaung, was now in utter ruin. It had been plundered and burnt by the Arakanese, and its surviving citizens sold into slavery. The Jesuits were convinced that this was "God's just way" of chastising these evil "barbarians for the enormous sins that were prevalent among them".

History books on this period invariably state that in 1600, a Portuguese adventurer named Felipe de Brito y Nicote, took advantage of the chaotic conditions and seized Syriam. But a little

Solid gold relics of the Mon Queen Bana Thau (r.1453-72) discovered in the relic chamber of a small pagoda by the Shwedagon in 1855. What remained of the collection is now in the Victoria and Albert Museum in London. From the *Journal of the Royal Asiatic Society* (1860).

အင်္ဂလိပ်များ၁၈၅၅ခုနှစ်တွင်
ဌာပနာဖေါက်ခါ
လန်ဒန်မြို့သို့ယူ ဆောင်သွားသော
မွန်ဘုရင် မကြီး ဘာနားသော်
(ရှင်စောပု) လှူဒန်းခဲ့သည့်
ရွှေသားပစ္စည်းများ

known Portuguese work entitled *A Brief Account of the Kingdom of Pegu in the East Indies, with the story of its Conquest,* said that it was Ribeyro de Souza, who, aided by an army of well-trained men, virtually controlled the Delta areas. He was so well organised and powerful that the Mon who had suffered intensely under the Burmese, invited him to be their ruler. As King Massinga [in Burmese Nga Zinga], he ruled for three years, and made a fortune by forcefully demanding customs tolls from vessels throughout the region.

The *Slapat Kyak Mah Tau* [History of the Kyak Mah Tau] of 1634, said that he removed the bejewelled finials from the Dagon shrine, and the Kyak Mah Tau at Pegu. Needless to say, the pagodas of Dagon and those of Syriam were the first to be looted. However, in 1603, due to a misunderstanding by the Viceroy of Goa, de Souza was replaced by Felipe de Brito y Nicote, who became a dominant figure in Lower Burma. Floris, who saw him in 1610, wrote that he "domineereth and careth for nobodie". From this time on the region was rarely at peace.

Judging by the information in the *Pawtugi Yazawin* [History of the Portuguese], one must assume that de Brito's success was due to his use of superior armaments. According to the account, his weapons included *"ga-ra-nat"* (a primitive form of the hand grenade), and *"bon"* (bomb). Encouraged by his priests, he tried to pressurise the local Buddhist population into becoming Catholics. Not content with despoiling the remaining pagodas, in 1612 he seized the huge bell, Ahwinga Sauk, from the Dagon Pagoda. His plan was to melt it down to make cannon, but the barge carrying it capsized and it fell into the Pazundaung Creek opposite Dawbon (a northern suburb of Rangoon); this great work of Mon art still rests at the bottom of the river, awaiting recovery.

In the same year, he and the Lord of Martaban sacked Toungoo, where Natshinnaung was now king, and brought him back to Syriam. Natshinnaung and de Brito were to become boon companions, and the former converted to Christianity. The taking of Toungoo by a foreigner so provoked the Burmese monarch Maha Dhamma Raja (r.1605-28) of Inn Wa, that he launched an attack on Syriam and captured it in 1613.

The king had the naked de Brito impaled on an iron spike in such a way that the vital organs were undamaged; the intention was to make sure that his victim lingered in prolonged agony as punishment for his sacrilegious acts. His beautiful wife, Donna Luisa de Saldana, niece of the Viceroy of Goa, was made to stand in the river for three days undergoing a ritual of cleansing, as the king wanted her for himself. But when she was brought to his bed chamber she confronted him with such contempt that he ordered her legs to be bored so that a cane loop could be inserted, and sent her to the capital, together with other captives, as a common slave. Meanwhile Natshinnaung, who had bludgeoned the old king of Pegu to death in 1603 and who was now considered a traitor, was executed by having his rib cage ripped open.

Maha Dhamma Raja later visited the Dagon Pagoda and dedicated four hundred and twenty men for its upkeep. He also had a large bell cast. In 1619, he offered a bejewelled finial on which were hung gold and silver bells donated by many of his courtiers.

The seventeenth century was a time of great natural disasters; so violent were the earthquakes and storms that the Dagon Pagoda was shattered on eight separate occasions. There was also constant civil unrest, rebellions, and invasions by the Chinese. Despite these unsettled times, and during a lull in the fighting in 1642, a history of the Dagon Pagoda was ordered to be prepared by Thalun (r.1629-48); this was undertaken by the abbots Anandadhaja and Anuruddha and was completed in May of that year.

Although Dagon was being included in the maps produced in the West, it was the port of Syriam which continued to be a centre of trade. Here the Portuguese, French, and later, the English, built sea-going vessels with teak, which was easily available and cheap. Syriam had become a large stockaded town ruled by a Burmese Governor, usually a trusted relation of the royal family.

During the 1470s, the Mon King Ramadhipatiraja had decreed that the official in charge of Lagun (Dagon) was to proceed in state, at the appropriate time to the Kyak Lagun, bearing twenty-five tree-shaped structures hung with offerings for the monks and the shrine; the tradition was followed by the Burmese dynasty which replaced his own. When Syriam became an important administrative centre, its Governor inherited this responsibility. On great feast days, the royal family sent down from the capital similar items, together with branches of gold and silver flowers, large gilded and silvered candles, rosaries, gold umbrellas, and pennants.

The *Thanlyin Yazawin* [History of Syriam], which was first compiled in 1650 and added to over the years, gives an interesting account of one of these annual processions. After crossing the river in his gilded state barge, which was accompanied by other vessels, the Governor of Syriam landed at Dagon. A procession was then formed, which consisted of his soldiers, and the men of the war boats, carrying spears, swords, and muskets. Behind them came the bearers of the official fans, and the state swords, which were wrapped in scarlet cloth. They were followed by the attendants of the household carrying betel boxes and other paraphernalia of rank. The Governor either rode on his elephant, or in a huge red palanquin, and was surrounded by his bodyguards. His principal wife did likewise followed by his junior wives and retainers in gaily decorated bullock carts.

The account also implies that the five guardian gods of the town which were once worshipped by the Mon during the fifteenth century, had been replaced by Maha Peinne (Ganesa, the elephant-headed Hindu god, and patron of traders). This deity must have been of some importance, for at the annual festival which was held at the end of December, a palanquin with seven roofs had to be built. The materials, such as wood, bamboo, gilt and coloured paper, together with all the necessary offerings had to be contributed by the merchants of Dagon. Later, musketeers, spearmen, swordsmen, boatmen, and all those in the employ of the Governor, placed the image in the palanquin and carried it around the town, accompanied by singers, dancers, and musicians.

Harvey, quoting Manucci, who was "writing in 1701-05, speaks of the Burmese governor's drinking feasts at the annual Shwedagon festival, where a law officer once got so drunk that for a bet he was fired into the air at the tail of a giant rocket, and his charred body was found next morning far away in the jungle".

By the early part of the eighteenth century, Syriam was ceasing to be a port. This was partly due to the numerous sandbanks which were becoming a threat to shipping. Dagon with its deep channel was now attracting the maritime trade. Nevertheless, the town had to wait until 1755 before it finally came into prominence.

On March 11 1752, Inn Wa, the Burmese capital of the Nyaungyan Dynasty (1599-1752), was sacked by the Mon, who were now enjoying a brief moment of power, and had established themselves at their former city of Pegu. Inn Wa was systematically looted and set ablaze, and the Burmese king, Mahadhammayaza Dipati (r.1733-52), and his entire court were brought down to the Mon capital. However, Aungzeya (r.1752-60), the headman of Moksobo (Shwebo) further north, declared himself king and as Alaungmintaya, successfully repulsed the invaders. Although the history books were to call him Alaungphaya, in his edicts this title is quite unknown. He always referred to himself as Alaungmintaya.

In the early 1750s, the town of Dagon was the scene of much bloodshed, being occupied in turn by the Mon and the Burmese. In April 1755 Alaungmintaya fought his way down to the Delta and captured Dagon. He visited the pagoda and prayed for success in crushing the Mon. At the shrine, he performed an elaborate religious ceremony, part of which entailed repeating a special Pali formula 1000 times. Assured by this ritual and in anticipation of an easy victory, on May 2 1755 he renamed the port Yangon or End of Threat (from the Mon). But eleven days later the Mon attacked, and there was a fierce battle in which the Burmese were victors. The monsoon season had begun and as there was further trouble in the north, the king had to hasten back to Upper Burma whilst the Mon were to make several brave yet fruitless attempts to regain their lost territories.

In 1756 Alaungmintaya returned from Shwebo to pray at the pagoda, and then proceeded to destroy Syriam which had become a Mon stronghold. The town fell to the Burmese on July 26 1756 and soon after French officers who had sided with the Mon were rounded up and executed. One in particular, called Bourno, was roasted alive. Alaungmintaya declared that henceforth Yangon was to be the chief port, and ordered the erection of a strong teak stockade around the town. A plan of the new port showed that it was virtually an island, with much of the marshy ground under water; during spring tides the river was said to rise by twenty-five to thirty feet.

On May 12 1757, the king seized Pegu and massacred many of its inhabitants, these included 3,000 Mon monks who were thrown to war-elephants which had been trained to kill. Alaungmintaya then came down to Yangon in July with the captive Mon royal family and treasure, and gave thanks at the Dagon Pagoda by building four massive pavilions and regilding the entire surface of the shrine. The king also took into service 400 men for the upkeep of the shrine. One of his henchmen, called U Shwe Ye, was appointed Governor, and with a guard of 3,570 men, was left to enforce law and order at Yangon.

Alaungmintaya passed through the town in December 1759, on his way to sack Ayutthaya. He again visited the pagoda and made sumptuous offerings, among which were four richly gilded *mahn-phaya*. These were lacquer images of the Buddha, each of which was moulded around one of the king's state robes. However, the king's ambitious campaign in Thailand was a disaster. While one account reported that he caught "a fever, and flux", most likely dysentery, which was effecting "one half of his forces", another said that he became ill "with consumption due to a venereal disease". Alaungmintaya died on May 11 1760 at Kin Ywa, miles from his beloved Shwebo. His corpse was brought to Yangon, and then taken up to the capital in a swiftly moving golden barge.

A work on the life of the Catholic Bishop Percoto, who was in the country for many years, said that in the environs of Yangon "crocodiles and elephants were common; and people [outside the stockade] built their houses on piles, not because of the waters, but for security against tigers". The surrounding jungle also contained wild boar, antelopes, and deer, while in the scrub and marshes, jungle fowl, snipe, woodcock, partridge, quail and a host of other birds were to be seen. Being Buddhists, many of the Burmese had an aversion to killing animals, and in a denigrating way called the Europeans who were grateful for this abundance of game, *hgnet-that* (killers of fowls).

By the 1750s, the cosmopolitan nature of Yangon, which was to be a prominent feature at the end of the nineteenth century, was already becoming evident. There were churches for the Christians, a Hindu temple, and a mosque for the followers of Islam. Although freedom of worship was tolerated by the Burmese, the same could not be said for the Christian missionaries.

In the 1760s, rivalry between the incumbents from the Italian and Portuguese religious establishments, who were known collectively to the Burmese as *bayingyi* (or Feringhi) came to a head, and one of the latter tried to poison his Italian counterpart. When that failed, the victim was attacked with a dagger. The priest was arrested and put on a vessel bound for India, but before departure decided to go for a swim in the river, and was promptly carried off by a large crocodile.

West of the Yangon stockade was a densely populated quarter known as Tatkalay whose occupants were connected with the marine trade. Living among them were a steadily growing community of Chinese merchants, and because of the junks in the vicinity, the landing stage came to be known to the Europeans as China Wharf. Unlike other foreign vessels, the junks were rarely over fifty tons, and therefore did not have to pay the tonnage duties and the port charges. The vessels also enjoyed the same status as native craft, which made the town a popular trading centre for the Chinese.

Tatkalay was also well known for its quarter reserved for the 'ladies of the night'. Its rival was the even more notorious Meinma Shun Ywa [Village of the Harlots] across the river at Maingthu, close to Dalla. Many of these unfortunate and helpless women were prisoners of their pimps, and had been either seized by the authorities because of their inability to pay taxes, or sold by their families to pay off debts. Foreign observers of the period noted that females outnumbered males in the country, and concluded that this was brought about by the numerous wars in which thousands of men had been killed.

In 1774, the Mon regiments which were in the service of Myaidu Min (r.1763-76), one of the sons of Alaungmintaya, mutinied, as they felt that they could no longer tolerate the brutal treatment they were receiving under Burmese rule. The mutineers, led by Bana Cin, created such havoc that their Burmese commanders had to flee to the safety of Yangon, with the Mon in hot pursuit. But the attackers failed to take it, and vented their frustration by setting fire to the outer town. On the arrival of strong reinforcements from the Burmese capital, the Mon soldiers gathered their families and escaped into Thailand. Those that remained foolishly believed that mercy would be shown but they were hunted out and massacred.

Several French ships which were unfortunate enough to have been in port at the time, and which were suspected of aiding the Mon, were seized by the Burmese. Their officers were tied hand and foot and thrown into the river, and their wives offered to the highest bidder. One young Frenchwoman who was raped by the Governor was sold by him the next day to an Armenian for the staggering price of 400 rupees; at the time a Thai female slave could be bought for five rupees.

In Upper Burma, Myaidu Min decided that it was time to crush Mon nationalistic feelings once and for all, and left his capital with his entire court for the Delta in January 1775. The royal progress in a huge flotilla of gilded barges, was supposedly to worship at the principal shrines along the Irrawaddy River and to place a jewelled finial on the Dagon Pagoda, but the real motive was more sinister. Myaidu Min intended to murder every male member of the Mon royal family, and thus deprive the Mon people of a figurehead around whom they could gather and plan further uprisings. To this end, the king brought with him Bana Drala (r.1747-57), the elderly ex-ruler of Pegu, who had been taken into captivity by Alaungmintaya in 1757; he and his family had been placed in close confinement at the capital, and forced to earn their living weaving baskets.

Myaidu Min arrived at Yangon at the end of February 1775, and for the duration of his visit, lived in a palace complex of wood and bamboo, west of the Dagon Pagoda. Earlier, work had begun on the rebuilding of the stupa which had been severely damaged during an earthquake in 1768. The structure was now raised to a height of 327 feet, and covered in gilding; the occasion was marked by theatricals and other entertainments. Arrangements were also made for the casting of a large bell to be called the Maha Ghanta; it was to be seven feet high, and six feet wide at the base.

At the end of the religious festivities, Myaidu Min exhibited to a specially collected crowd of Mon "their venerated monarch, bound in fetters, and bowed down with years and anguish, by exposing him as a public malefactor, to suffer under the stroke of the common executioner" - a deliberate insult to a crowned head of state; until then, it had always been the rule among the Mon and Burmese that royal blood was never shed; the victims were usually put into velvet sacks and drowned.

After a mock trial in which Bana Drala was supposedly found guilty of instigating the recent rebellion by the Mon, he was taken with other prisoners to Awabauk and beheaded on March 15 1775. After the execution it was discovered that the corpse had a ball of wax clutched in its hand. When opened it was found to contain a huge ruby, which was sent immediately to the king.

The fleet of vessels which carried Myaidu Min and his court left Yangon for Inn Wa in May 1775. He died in June 1776 from a mysterious illness; one account which was recorded by a Burmese court official who later defected to the Thai, claimed that the king "became ill of venereal disease". Yet, despite the tragic death of Bana Drala, the Mon were prepared to fight on for their independence. They had become so traumatised that many desperately believed and took comfort in the rumours that a powerful figure, known as Smin Mon [King Mon] was about to appear and deliver them from the cruelties of the Burmans.

In 1782, a fisherman named Nai Chien presented himself as the deliverer of the Mon people and collected a large body of men. He attacked the office of the Governor of Yangon, killing several officials. However, the rebels, many of whom were simple villagers, were soon overpowered and 500 of the Mon inhabitants from in and around the town were rounded up and put to death.

Under Badon Min (r.1782-1819), the Burmese became aware of the need to increase foreign trade and encouraged aliens to settle at their chief port. Many of these merchants were "Armenians, Parsees, and Mussulmen" from India, and some Europeans, who because of their astuteness and knowledge of the outside world acquired much wealth. Among them, a Muslim trader who converted to Buddhism, a rare event and one punishable by death in an Islamic State, was credited with having constructed a well-built road leading from the landing stage to the Dagon Pagoda; this was along the ancient Pilgrim's Way.

The Chinese, to whom the port of Yangon was known as Yen-kung from as early as 1777, were fully aware of its strategic position and of the enormous profits to be made from the country's products; variants in the name of the town were to evolve from Yang-kung to Yang-kang. By the 1790s, the Chinese merchants who had come from such places as Fukien, Kuangtung (Canton), and the Straits of Malacca, had become extremely prosperous. They brought with them silks, porcelain, and gold. This last item was in ever increasing demand by the Burmese; one of the main uses being the annual regilding of the thousands of images and pagodas throughout the land.

At the time, a foreign vessel could not enter the river leading to the port without a native pilot. When it finally anchored at a designated wharf, one of its officers had to present himself at the office of the Governor with a list of its cargo. The ships' cannon, muskets, and the rudder had to be taken ashore. A duty of twelve and a half percent was then paid, ten percent of which was sent to the capital, a journey which sometimes took nearly six weeks by water; the rest was divided between the Governor and his officials.

Among the items being exported from Yangon was the famous teak, which was sent either as planks, or ready-made masts for ships. This was followed by cutch, lac, isinglass, vegetable oil, and petroleum. Although gold and precious stones were forbidden to be taken out of the country, these items were nevertheless smuggled out after appropriate bribes had been offered to the officials. Foreign merchants were sometimes obliged to spend their profits on repairs to their vessels, or on building a new one. It was said that on the completion of a vessel, it was not advisable to linger in port, for the river was infested with a marine worm which had a habit of boring into wood. Nevertheless, the dockyards were kept busy, and sea going vessels of up to 900 tons were being built by Burmese carpenters who had trained under Europeans.

During the period of Symes's visit, Tatkalay still had its street of prostitutes, and its rival across

... *along the bank of the river about a mile in breadth. The city or miou is a square surrounded by a high stockade, and on the North side it is further strengthened by an indifferent fosse, across which a wooden bridge is thrown; in this face there are two gates, in each of the others only one. Wooden stages are erected in several places within the stockade, for the musketeers to stand on in case of an attack.*

On the south side, towards the river, which is about twenty or thirty yards from the palisade, there are a number of huts and three wharfs with cranes for landing goods. A battery of twelve cannons, six and nine pounders, raised on the bank, commands the river; but the guns and carriages are in such a wretched condition that they could do little execution. Close to the principal wharf are two commodious wooden houses, used by the merchants as an exchange, where they usually meet in the cool of the morning and evening; to converse and transact business.

The streets of the town are narrow, but clean and well paved; there are numerous channels to carry off the rain, over which strong planks are laid, to prevent an interruption of intercourse. The houses are raised on posts from the ground; the smaller supported by bamboos, the larger by strong timbers. All the officers of Government, the most opulent merchants and persons of consideration, live within the fort; shipwrights and people of inferior rank, inhabit the suburbs.

The houses were composed of such combustible materials, the inhabitants are under continual dread of fire, against which they take every precaution. The roofs are lightly covered and at each door stands a long bamboo with an iron hook at the end to pull down the thatch. There is also another pole with a grating of iron at the extremity about three feet square, to suppress flames by pressure. Almost every house had earthen pots filled with water on the roof, and a particular class of people called pagwet whose business it is to prevent and extinguish fires perambulate the streets during the night.

Pigs roamed about the town at large; these animals which are with reason held unclean, so do not belong to any particular owners; they are servants of the public, common scavengers; they go under the houses and devour the filth. The Burmans are also fond of dogs, numbers of which infest the streets; the breed is small and extremely noisy.

MICHAEL SYMES, EMBASSY TO THE COURT OF AVA, 1795.

"A Bazaar in Burmah" showing the numerous racial types. A policemen with his spear stands on the left. *The Graphic*, May 22 1875.

ကိုလိုနီ ခေတ် မြန်မာဈေး ရွာခင်း

... the town has a rude appearance from the river, being composed of straggling huts of cadjan and bamboo, raised on piles close to the water's edge, slips for building ships, and mud docks. Some few tiled houses are seen among the trees within the stockade, and the roof of the custom-house is raised two stories in the Chinese-style; part of the timber stockade, which encloses what is called the fort, is seen towards the river; and near the flag-staff is a very good wooden pier, with a crane, and steps for landing goods, etc., Here also is placed the saluting battery, on which is mounted sixteen old iron guns, four or six pounders, which are run out through port-holes, in a wooden breast-work, like a ship's side. Many small pagodas, some of them with gilt spires, are seen amongst the trees on both sides of the river. The buildings along shore, on the town side, extend about one mile and a half, and on the opposite one, about a quarter of a mile.

In the vicinity of the town are several orchards of fruit trees, and many pleasant situations for building. The air is pure and elastic, and as yet I have not found the heat oppressive. The general salubrity of the air is best evinced by its effects; the inhabitants, male and female, are a hale robust race; and strangers in general preserve their health, or recover soon if they arrive sick.

HIRAM COX, 1796.

the river continued as a place of notoriety. He commented that those who "follow this course of life are not at their own disposal nor receive the earnings of their unhappy profession. They are slaves sold to a licensed pander for debts more frequently contracted by others than by themselves". He also added that the "lower class of Burmans make no scruple of selling their daughters, and even their wives, to foreigners who come to pass a temporary residence amongst them. It reflects no disgrace on any of the parties and the woman is not dishonoured by the connection".

Foreigners in town consisted of Moguls, Malabars, Persians, Parsees, Armenians, Portuguese, French, and English. Symes noted that "the members of this discordant multitude are not only permitted to reside under the protection of government but likewise enjoy the most liberal toleration in matters of religion". It was not unusual to see processions from the various religious denominations passing down the same street on their way to their respective places of worship. During Symes's visit, a Portuguese named Jhansi was the Akaukwun (Collector of Revenue) and tried his best to improve facilities in the town with paved streets, bridges, a large brick customhouse and impressive wharf. But being uneducated and barely able to speak the Burmese language, he was held in derision by the locals. The Armenian community were mainly merchants, led by Baba-Sheen, who later became the Akaukwun. He was said to have hated the English, and went out of his way to make mischief between the two nations.

Hiram Cox who arrived in 1796 described a waterfall in the vicinity of the Shwedagon Pagoda that was situated "in a fork between two of these ridges, the water during the rains forces a passage, and forms a cascade of about 14 feet perpendicular", and observed that it had scooped out a deep basin in the rock; the waterfall no longer exists.

Despite its mean appearance, the town certainly knew how to entertain visiting envoys. At his official reception, Cox mentions that "Mr. Jhansey the Shabunder, and Baba-Sheen [an Armenian] the collector of the revenues of the province, the two superior members of government here, received me at the pier-head. From thence I proceeded through an avenue formed by the inhabitants seated on the ground, (preceded by the officer of the police to preserve order), towards the house provided for my residence. On passing the custom-house, a band of musicians, dancers, exhibited for my entertainment; and, at the head of the principal street, another band of Siamese dancers were stationed. I stopped for a few minutes to observe them; some were gaudily dressed, as females, in velvet brocade with gold ornaments, according to the fashion of the country; the dancing consisted of various attitudes, and beating time to a slow measure with their feet".

Cox was fortunate to witness the Tasaungdaing festivities (Festival of Lights) on the Dagon Pagoda, and saw great crowds of people in their gala clothes, carrying offerings for the shrine. The numerous processions and pageants which were accompanied by bands of musicians, dancers and singers, consisted of huge animals and other exotic creatures made of brightly coloured paper, tinsel, and bamboo. He added that the "manners of the whole reflected credit upon them as a nation; no jostling, or ill-humour was seen, all were gay and decorous". Although shoes were not permitted on the pagoda platform, he saw that several Europeans and native Christians ignored this ruling, which showed extraordinary tolerance on the part of the Burmese. The evening ended with a firework display.

According to other European observers, by the early 1800s, Yangon appears to have slipped into squalor, and is often described as a "dirty little town". Contemporary sketches show flimsy houses of wood and bamboo, and few brick buildings. Even the 'palace' of the governor was of wood, and said to have been crudely built. But this was in line with the strict sumptuary laws prevalent at the time; only royalty and the senior members of the priesthood were allowed carved and gilded residences. The town also attracted hardened criminals and undesirable Europeans from India, and other parts of the East; such characters were to pose a problem to the authorities.

On the other hand, Vincentius Sangermano, the Italian Barnabite priest, whose Order had been in Burma since 1728, saw the town in a different light, and said that it was a thriving port. He added that there were two Catholic churches:

Burmese Ear Boring Festival

...the dancer was a girl of about ten years of age, who kept excellent time to the music, with various inflexions of her body, and graceful movements of her arms and hands, and occasionally with her feet. To my taste this was the best dancing I had ever seen among the natives of India, being both graceful and decorous; and the music, although some of the instruments were rather harsh to an European ear, yet on the whole produced a pleasing effect.

HIRAM COX, 1796.

Right: Burmese dancers performing at a private function. The small orchestra on the right is composed of wind, string, and percussion instruments. c.1900.

၁၉၀၀ခုနှစ်လောက်တွင် နာမည်ကျော်ကြားသော အငြိမ့်လောကမှ ဆိုင်တီ၊ကအနုပညာ ရှင်ကြီ များ

Burmese Dance.

No 27

one in the city, dedicated to the Assumption of the Blessed Virgin, made in wood and according to the style of the country, and with room enough for one thousand people; the other was two miles out of the city [at Tatkalay] and dedicated to Saint John the Baptist, made of bricks and cement and bigger than the first.

Sangermano was the parish priest of the latter, which was built in the European style. There was a school for orphaned girls, and another for boys. In the latter, he taught subjects such as "grammar, rhetoric, philosophy, mathematics, navigation, and theology". The "able pilots, engineers, and experts in other sciences" of the town, are said to have owed their knowledge to his teaching. Sangermano prepared the first detailed chart of the port for the East India Company, from whom he received a pension.

Next to the school was a large brick hospital with two dormitories, where he acted as physician, and was helped by a group of Burmese widows. At the time, the port was ruled by a Viceroy, and he and his pious lady, who were both Buddhists, showed great kindness to the Catholic community, and regularly contributed incense and candles for the church; she was said to have been taken by the rituals of the church, and sometimes attended Mass with her suite. In 1810, although a great fire destroyed most of the town, the two churches, hospital, and schools were saved.

However, by 1813, the friendly attitude of the Burmese Government had changed. At court, anti-foreign feeling ran high, and a policy which did not help either business or trade was encouraged. In the Delta regions there were outbreaks of cholera and famine, murders and robberies. The situation was said to have been particularly bad in and around the town. This led to brutal measures having to be taken by the authorities. When apprehended, criminals were beheaded and their bodies left "on the roadside with their backs upward, their decapitated heads being reversed and fastened to the ground by wooden pins driven through their mouths".

The official badge of the executioner consisted of a red cloth tied across his chest; other distinguishing marks were the large black circle on each cheek, and the word *lu-that* (murderer) tattooed on his forehead. For serious crimes death was slow and lingering. The executioner, gripping a long sword with both hands, would move back about twenty yards and then make a rush at his victim, slashing open his chest and stomach; no attempts were made to put him out of misery.

It would appear that nothing was done by those in authority to reclaim the land around the town, which was low-lying and criss-crossed by small creeks which flooded at high tide. This was in total contrast to the surrounding countryside with its numerous farms, well-stocked orchards of palm, plantains, jack-fruit, custard apple, and pineapples. Members of the simple farming communities which consisted of Burmese, Karens, Mon, and Shan, certainly left a good impression on the foreign observers.

Henry Gouger, the young English merchant who visited Burma in 1822, however was extremely uncomplimentary about the port, and was appalled at the shabby conditions. He noted that it was inhabited by between "8,000 to 10,000 people, the houses being built of bamboo and teak planks with thatched roofs", and that it had a "mean, uninviting appearance, but it was the seat of government of an extensive Province, ruled over by a Viceroy, a Woongee of

The old south entrance to the Shwedagon Pagoda. The brick gateway with the two shrines and demon guardians was built by King Tharrawaddy (r.1837-46) during his state visit to Rangoon in 1841. Photographed sometime before 1887. In that year several interconnected pavilions were built which covered the stairs almost down to the main road.

၁၈၈၇ခုနှစ်မတိုင်မီရိုက်ကူး ထာ သော ရွှေတိဂုံတောင်ဖက်မုတ်၊ သာယာဝတီမင် ကောင် မူ

the Empire, in high favour at the Court", whose seat was usually at Pegu. Gouger met the Governor of Yangon in his "gloomy palace", and was a little unnerved to see him wandering about with a long lance in his hand; a habit which inspired fear in many with whom he came into contact. But it turned out he was extremely helpful to Gouger.

The Akaukwun or Collector of Taxes and Customs at the time was a Spaniard called Lanciego. Although a foreign vessel was still obliged to surrender its rudder and weapons, this stipulation could be evaded by substantial bribes to the Akaukwun and others. Gouger added that as the officials were not paid by the Crown, they had to obtain their salaries in whatever way they could. As a result, corruption was rampant.

Gouger had nothing but praise for the ordinary Burmese, and said that the people were kind and hospitable, and did not suffer from the prejudices of caste, and that freedom was "allowed to their women, who are never secluded" and that they were free from the "obsequious manners of the natives of British India". But this behaviour was only among themselves, and foreigners with

A Burmese minister of high rank and attendant. The official robe was of red velvet, with a border of Banares brocade, the richness and width increasing with seniority. Also worn was a headdress which was of velvet, decorated with bands, flowers, and leaf shapes of beaten gold. c. early 1870s.

၁၈၇၀ခုနှစ်လောက်တွင် ရတနာပုံရွှေမြို့ တော်ကြီ ၌အမှုတော်ထမ် ခဲ့သော ဝန်ရှင်မင် ကြီ

... the Emperor gives no salaries to the Mandarins; indeed before any one can obtain the dignity, he must spend large sums in presents; and in order to maintain himself in it, still larger ones are necessary, not only to the Emperor, but also to his queens and to all the principal personages about the court. To this must be added the expenses of these grandees in their houses, dress, and equipages, which must be proportional to their dignity; and when we consider that the money for all this must be furnished by the people under their care, it will easily be imagined, what dreadful oppression is put in practice to draw it from them...extortions and oppressions of which I have spoken, are nothing in comparison to those practised by the Mandarins in the provincial cities, and above all, in Rangoon. For this city, being situated at a great distance from the court, is more exposed to their rapacity.

VINCENTIUS SANGERMANO, 1893.

whom they felt themselves on equal terms. Their attitude, however, changed dramatically when they came in contact with the governing classes. He noted that "submission, even to obsequiousness, is inflexibly demanded by one, and yielded by the other from motives of fear". Gouger was amazed at the transformation in character of a "plebeian" who had come to power; he at once assumed the arrogance and "tyranny of office with as much apparent ease as if it had been his birthright".

Many of the Europeans and the American missionaries of this period tended to depict the Burmese, especially the ruling classes, in an unfavourable light. Some of the worse offenders in this category being the Judsons, to whom the Burmese were always the 'barbaric heathens'. The many good qualities which are inherent among Buddhists, and which these uninvited foreigners experienced were rarely acknowledged, or else grudgingly mentioned. Anna Judson, in particular, with much wringing of hands was the one who supposedly 'suffered' most terribly in this land which was "full of darkness and idolatry". However, Helen Trager's *Burma Through Alien Eyes* a brilliantly revealing work, will no doubt alter the vision one has held of these oh-so-pious and long-suffering missionaries who probably had an unconscious wish for martyrdom.

The nineteenth century was to see three separate head-on collisions between the British in India and the Burmese. Fiercely independent, inward looking, ignorant of the outside world and deluded by some of their fawning advisors who only had their own interests at heart, the often naive Lords of the Golden Palace were powerless to stop the gradual fragmentation of their once vast kingdom.

The Combustible Commodore

CLASH WITH THE
EAST INDIA COMPANY
1824-1852

The first encounter with the East India Company occurred in Arakan during the closing years of Badon Min's reign. A letter, written in the usual tremble and obey style by Naymyo Thura, Governor of Yamawaddy (Ramree), an island off Arakan, threatening to come in person and annihilate the British was received by the Governor General of India. The tense situation was to smoulder on for several years under his grandson, Sagaing Min (r.1819-37), only to burst into a full-scale war in 1824. Judging by the numerous pompous sounding titles, like King of Kings or Lord of the Universe, with which these rulers styled themselves, the atmosphere at court was so deluded that throughout the hostilities, the British, who were thought to be no better than belonging to a vassal race, were referred to as *kala-thabon* (foreign rebels).

On May 11 1824, British war ships, guided by the towering golden mass of the Dagon Pagoda, appeared before Yangon. After a brief exchange, which lasted about twenty minutes, the stockaded town was taken. As the entire area had been evacuated earlier by the Burmese authorities, there were no casualties among the civilian inhabitants. The defenders who were quite unprepared did not offer very much resistance and promptly fled into the surrounding jungle.

One British observer added that "in whatever virtues

Left: A bejewelled Burmese lady holding a 'whacking great charoot'. Her open-fronted jacket which is based on the court style is of foreign lace and has been decorated with two triangular pieces in front called *kalama-no* (Indian women's breasts). The elaborate horizontal ah-cheik wave patterns of the traditional *htamein* (skirt) have been replaced by what was considered to be a modern design of vertical stripes. c.1890s.

ဆေး လိပ်ကိုအပေါ်လုပ်ခါ ငယ်ချစ်မောင်
ကိုရွှေဘိန် အာ မျှော်နေရှာသော ရွှေဂုံသူ

Above: The Pilgrim's Way (now called Shwedagon Pagoda Road) leading to the south entrance of the great shrine. Late 1860s. From Albert Fytche's Burma Past and Present.

၁၈၆၀ခုနှစ်လောက်မှ ရွှေတိဂုံဘုရား လမ်း ရှုခင်း

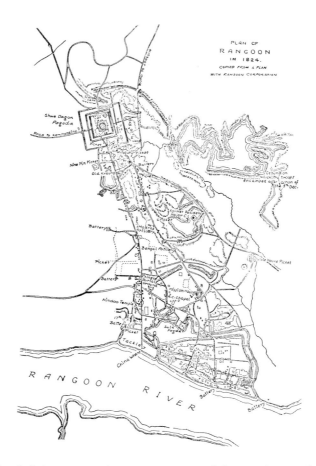

the Birmese may be deficient, certainly courage is not of the number; and as soon as their first emotions of astonishment had subsided, they prepared all hazards for a resolute and a patriotic defence", the most intimidating of which being the huge fire rafts which were sent down with the ebb tide. Some consisted of as many as forty canoes on which were placed jars of blazing crude oil; the loosely tied canoes were designed to wrap themselves around a vessel.

Unfortunately for the British, the monsoon season had begun, and the rain fell "in such quantity, that it was impossible for our troops to keep the field and act upon a regular system. Harassed, too, by continuous incursions of the enemy, threatened with an approaching famine, and reduced by an epidemic, which broke out amongst them to a state of the greatest debility". As a result the British were confined to the town and its vicinity for nearly eight months.

A British military map of 1824 indicates that the central and administrative sector of the town was completely surrounded by water, with the additional protection of a stockade. The area of habitation was widest at the eastern end and gradually tapered almost to a point towards the west. It was in fact an artificially created island which was connected to the rest of the town by numerous bridges. The largest expanse of water, which appeared to be a tidal lagoon, was in the area of the Sule Pagoda, and was connected to the main river by two creeks. Further inland there were isolated stretches of water which, judging by their formation, must once have been part of another large creek, that had been filled in at some time in the past. The ground to the north of the town was covered in numerous mounds and hillocks on which pagodas and monasteries had been built.

The map also depicts embankments all around the irregularly shaped edges of the large expanse of water, which was later to be known as the Royal Lakes, indicating that attempts had been made in the past to retain the water; the lake appears to have been fed by several springs

…approach to it on the south face, is through fine rows of mango, cocoa-nut, and other beautiful trees leading from the town, and shading a capital road, at each side of which are monasteries, or kioums, of great antiquity, and carved all over with curious images and ornaments, whilst every now and then the attention is attracted by huge images of griffins [chinthe-leogryphs] and other hideous monsters, guarding the entrance to different pagodas. At the end of this road rises, abruptly, the eminence on which the Dagon stands.

…ascending the steps, which are very dark, you suddenly pass through a small gate, and emerge into the upper terrace, where the great pagoda, at about fifty yards distance, rears its lofty head in perfect splendour. This immense octagonal gilt-based monument is surrounded by a vast number of smaller pagodas, griffins, sphinxes, and images of the Burman deities. The height of the tee [finial], three hundred and thirty-six feet from the terrace, and the elegance with which this enormous mass is built, combine to render it one of the grandest and most curious sights a stranger can notice. From the base it assumes the form of a ball, or a dome, and then gracefully tapers to a point of considerable height, the summit of which is surmounted by a tee, or umbrella, of open iron-work, from whence are suspended a number of small bells, which are set in motion by the slightest breeze, and produce a confused though not unpleasant sound.

TRANT, TWO YEARS IN AVA, 1827.

THE BURMESE WAR.—THE DAGON PAGODA, AT RANGOON.—(SEE NEXT PAGE.)

"The Dagon Pagoda at Rangoon". Sections of the stockade can still be seen. The scene shows that the south-eastern terrace of the stupa was covered in small pagodas; several thousand could be seen all over Rangoon. By 1855, all had been demolished to make way for the contonment. *The Illustrated London News*, December 4, 1852.

၁၈၅၂ခုနှစ်မှရွှေတိဂုံခင် ၊ ထိုအချိန်၌ ရန်ကုန်မြို့ပေါ်တွင်စေတီငယ်ထောင်ပေါင် များစွာ ရှိခဲ့သည်ဟု အင်္ဂလိပ်စါရေ့ဆရာ တစ်ဦး ကဆိုခဲ့သည်

...arms of the soldiery are muskets (without bayonets), swords and spears; they carry their powder in a horn, and sometimes in a dried pumpkin [gourd], or a long cloth bag. The weapon they use best is the ginjal, or swivel, which they fire with precision. The dah, or sword, is used for building their houses, fighting, or preparing their food. The handle is of the same length as the blade; so that they can hold it with one or both hands, and strike a powerful blow with it. Those of the chiefs are cased in gold or silver, and covered with gems. Their spears are ornamented with horse-hair; they have also a kind of javelin, which is thrown from the back of an elephant, by means of a small crooked stick, in a manner similar to that practiced by natives of New South Wales.

The Burmese war canoes were rowed or paddled by thirty or forty men, their weapons placed at their side; they carry also a few soldiers, with a piece of ordnance mounted on the prow, which is made sharp, for the purpose of running down and staving smaller craft.

JAMES ALEXANDER, 1825-26

"Explosion of the Expense magazine, and destruction of the strong stockade by a shell from the squadron". This was triggered off by a shot from the warship *Sesostris* and also destroyed the King's Wharf. On the left are the pagodas of Dalla, none exists today. *The Illustrated London News.* June 26 1852.

၁၈၅၂ခုနှစ်တွင် ရန်ကုန်သစ်တပ်ကိုအင်္ဂလိပ်တပ်များ တိုက်ခိုက်နေကြပုံ

along the ridge leading to the Dagon Pagoda, and also by a tidal stream. This large expanse of water was believed to date from the fifteenth and sixteenth centuries, when the Mon excavated the clay deposits for making bricks, or to fill in the deep ravines near the great pagoda. Only three roads are discernible. The most prominent being the main avenue, or Pilgrim's Way, which led to the Dagon Pagoda from what was called China Wharf. This was in the quarter known as Tatkalay. It is possible that this road was already in existence from the time of the Mon kings and was the one mentioned by Gasparo Balbi in 1583. Although all three roads began from the riverside, two of them later merged at the foot of the pagoda and continued northwards.

According to Crawfurd, the British envoy, the town and suburbs extended "about a mile along the bank of the river, and are in depth about three-quarters of a mile; but the houses are very unequally scattered over this area. The fort, or stockade, is an irregular square; the north and south faces of which were found to measure 1145 yards; the east, 598; and the west, 197. On the north face there are two gates and a sally-port; on the south, three gates and three sally-ports; on the east, two gates; and on the west, one gate and one sally-port. The stockade is fourteen feet high, and is composed of heavy beams of teak timber. It has in some places a stage to fire musquetry from, in the parapet over which are a kind of embrasures, loop-holes. On the south side there is a miserable ditch, and in one situation a deep swamp, both overgrown with Arums, Pontiderias, the Pitsia stratiota and other aquatic plants. Over the ditch there is a causeway, and over the marsh a long wooden bridge, connecting one of the gates with a large temple [Sule Pagoda] and monastery."

"Rangoon and its suburbs are divided into eight wards, called, in the Burman language, *yat*, superintended by an officer called the *yat-gaong*, whose business is to maintain watch and ward within his division. The palisaded fort, or stockade, which is properly what the Burmans denominate a town or *myo*, is composed of three wide and clean streets running east and west, and three smaller ones crossing them and fronting the gates of the south face. The most populous part of the town is the suburb called Taklay, immediately on the west face of the stockade".

The First Anglo-Burmese War was not confined only to the Delta regions, but was also being conducted more successfully in Tenasserim, with a Colonel Miles in command. In October 1824, all Yangon flocked to see the magnificent Burmese state carriage which had been taken, together with other booty, at the capture of Tavoy, earlier on September 9. The vehicle, described as a Rath (in Burmese *yet-htar*) had been intended for Sagaing Min (r.1819-37) and was sumptuously carved and gilded. Documents connected with its construction indicated that a total of 20,000 precious stones had been used to decorate it. Also captured were the Viceroy of Tavoy and his son; both are said to have surrendered their silver-mounted swords of state. According to *The Mirror*, the former was a man of "great personal strength, and unbounded ferocity" and had earlier been responsible for the death of a Thai prince whom he had taken prisoner; after being tortured, the man had been left in an iron cage and starved. The carriage, the value of which was estimated at the time at the huge sum of £12,500 did not stay in Yangon for long, for it was taken together with the other treasures to Calcutta. Also taken were the Viceroy and his iron cage. On arrival, the vehicle was sold to an entrepreneur who had it shipped to London and subsequently exhibited at the Egyptian Hall in Piccadilly. The exhibition also included Burmese works of art, the Viceroy's silver spear, and the first set of musical instruments to be seen in the West. In the Delta regions, and along the Irrawaddy River, there was continuous fighting throughout 1825, and until April 1 of that year, the Burmese forces were led by the celebrated General Maha Bandula.

During the British occupation of Yangon, incalculable damage was done to the centuries-old Buddhist shrines and monasteries; the latter from which the monks had been ejected were used as quarters for the British Army. An officer even had his charpoy (bed) placed in the lap of one of the larger images, while others stuck pipes in the smiling mouths of Buddhas - a shocking sight to devout Buddhists. The numerous monastic libraries were also looted. An extract from a letter which appeared in *The Mirror* said that "when the Burmese temples and monasteries were ransacked by our soldiers, they strewed about the books found there, as useless lumber". Thousands of valuable manuscripts were thus lost, and a few taken away as souvenirs.

British and Indian soldiers also broke into and vandalized the many gilded pagodas built along the roads leading to the great pagoda, and on the main terrace itself. The Muslim soldiers belonging to the British Army were particularly destructive, being iconoclasts they took a great delight in mutilating and knocking off the heads of thousands of images. A Lieutenant Havelock who billeted his men in the sumptuously carved and gilded prayer halls, referred to the sacred mount as that "haughty hill of devil worship". Trant, on the other hand, who was awed by the beauty of the Dagon Pagoda, has left a vivid description of it (above).

While some of the officers, such as the writer James Alexander, were appalled at the desecration, others, like General Campbell encouraged his men to tunnel into the base of the Dagon Pagoda in search of the fabled riches hidden there. Fortunately, they were unsuccessful in finding the hoard. Scott O'Connor noted in his *Silken East* that "a cutting made into its centre has revealed the fact that the original pagoda had seven casings added to it before it attained its present proportions." Alexander mentions that all "the smaller temples (of which there are several thousand) have been picked by the Europeans for the sake of the small silver Gaudmas. Few steps were taken to check this culpable practice". Only about ten large pagodas were to survive the British demolition teams of the early 1850s. He added that it was "truly melancholy to observe the ravages which had been committed on the smaller pagodas surrounding the Shoe [Shwe] Dagoon." It would appear that it was from about this time that the word *shwe* (golden) prefixed the word *dagon,* and the pagoda came to be known as the Shwedagon.

A number of personal accounts and illustrations of the period speak of and depict ruined temples and Buddhas with gaping holes. The author, George Bird, writing in 1896, said that the octagonal Sule Pagoda assumed its present height of 152 feet sometime in 1826. This would imply that this venerated Mon shrine, whose original shape and dimensions will now never be known, did not escape the attentions of the British soldiers; its relic chambers doubtless held artifacts of priceless archaeological importance. One must assume that the structure was so damaged that it had to be rebuilt by some devout Buddhist. In a map of the town dated 1824, a large lake almost surrounds the shrine, and access to the eastern entrance was by a wide wooden causeway.   The earliest view of the Sule Pagoda (half-hidden by trees) appears in J Grierson's *Twelve Select Views of the Seat of War.*

This type of vandalism, however, was not confined only to the invading foreigners; during unsettled times, the Burmese, Mon, and other ethnic groups also indulged in this easy way of acquiring wealth. If caught, the penalty for this sacrilege was usually death by impalement, and the corpse was put on display for three days. Trant said that there was a railed enclosure in town

A Burmese youth with tattoos. Before taking the picture, the photographer highlighted the tattoo patterns with white paint, as the original designs which were black would not have been discernible against the dark brown skin. Beato.c.1890s. ထို ကွင် မင်ကြောင်နှင့် မြန်မာသာ ကောင် ရတနာတစ်ဦ

… born a soldier, the Burmese is accustomed, from his earliest years to consider war and foreign conquest as his trade…When engaged in offensive warfare the Burmese is arrogant, bold and daring: possessed of strength and activity superior to all his neighbours, and capable of enduring great fatigue, his movements are rapid, and his perseverance in overcoming obstacles, almost irresistible: possessed, too, of a superior science and ability in their peculiar system of fighting, he has seldom met his equal in the field, or even experienced serious resistance in the numerous conquests which of later years had been added to the empire.

SNODGRASS, NARRATIVE OF THE BURMESE WAR, 1827.

where executions were carried out, which were attended by large crowds, many of whom were forced by the authorities to be present, as a warning.

Crawfurd described the execution of four men who had been accused of this type of crime. He said that they had "their abdomens laid open; huge gashes were cut in their sides and limbs, laying bare the bones; and one individual, whose crime was deemed of a more aggravated nature than that of the rest, had a stake driven through his chest".

Europeans were amazed at the way most Burmans suffered death with total indifference; being Buddhists, the attitude was that it must have been their fate to die this way, and that there was nothing they could do about it. One onlooker saw a deserter, after the "executioner had performed more than half his task", eat a banana with his bowels hanging out. Another smoked a cheroot while waiting patiently for his turn. This curious characteristic, when primed with alcohol or drugs, was to produce formidable fighting men whose blind bravery of the 'kamikaze' type was often spoken of with admiration by the British. Yet conscripts who were dragged from their rice fields, and mountain villages, did not go willingly to battle. Crawfurd was told of the arrival in town of hundreds of these untrained men who were tied hand and foot, herded like cattle, and sent off to the war zones in crowded boats.

The First Anglo-Burmese War was to continue into the early part of 1826. Among the Burmese, the morale of the royal army had taken a plunge since the tragic death of the famous Maha Bandula on April 1 1825. Nevertheless they fought on bravely with their antiquated weapons and a desire to preserve their independence. But circumstances were against them; for years, unscrupulous dealers, among them British and Indian, had been selling arms of a doubtful quality to the unsuspecting Burmese. Many of the guns were rejects from the British army in India, and were said to have been dangerous. The author, Captain Marryat, who was present at the taking of Yangon, had nothing but praise for the Burmese who held out for nearly three years, with only inadequate weapons to assist them. He declared that they lost the war only because of the superiority of British arms.

It would appear that the Burmese had sympathisers in unexpected quarters, who knew that bravery alone was no match against the discipline and modern weapons possessed by the British Army. In January 1826 a mysterious ship which was later identified as being American was spotted in the Gulf of Martaban and was chased and captured by a British man-of-war. On being boarded it was discovered to be loaded with "arms and warlike stores" intended for the Burmese Governor.

The First Anglo-Burmese War ended with the signing of the Yandabo Treaty on February 24 1826. Sagaing Min ceded to the East India Company, Arakan and Tenasserim, and gave up all claims to Assam, Cachar, and Manipur; a heavy indemnity was also demanded. The British were to retain the port and 100 miles of territory surrounding it, until the instalments of the indemnity were delivered by the Burmese court. This was a terrible personal blow for Sagaing Min, who was by nature prone to violent mood swings. He never quite recovered from the humiliation and gradually slipped into a deep depression, occasionally emerging from this unfortunate state to perform essential ceremonial and religious duties.

Despite their victory, the British losses were heavy. At the beginning of the war, the retreating Burmese army had seen to it that food supplies could not be obtained locally. Due to an inadequate supply of medicine, provisions, and the intemperate climate, it was claimed that among the first batch of European troops which consisted of 3,586 men, 3,115 died of disease; the Indian regulars also suffered heavy losses. In all, a total of fifteen thousand men died; the cost of the war was stated to have been over £13,000,000. As a result of the unsettled state of the country farmers were unable to work their fields, causing a great famine. The price of rice rose to such an extent that only the wealthy could afford it while the majority of the people had to rely on whatever could be procured from the jungle; many starved. Added to this was a new threat in the form of numerous hungry tigers which carried off cattle and humans alike. The tigers became so bold that they took to prowling near the town in broad daylight; several were killed in the town itself.

For the survivors in the British army, grain from India, and the sudden appearance of junks from Penang loaded with fresh provisions, must have seemed like manna from heaven. This much needed sustenance was bought up by the military authorities. Fortunately, the food situation began to improve as people began returning from their hiding places in the jungle to their villages. In town, religious festivals were again being celebrated, these were invariably accompanied by theatrical shows, music and dancing.

Throughout this period, the more affluent among the European officers bought themselves a temporary Burmese 'wife'; the price varied between fifty and sixty rupees. It was no doubt a prudent move; as this was a busy port, contact with the common prostitutes would have been hazardous. Burmese girls were astute enough to realise that a 'red coat' (a soldier) was poor, but a liaison with an Englishman in a 'dark coat' (a civil servant or merchant) held better prospects.

Under the British, temporary military rule was imposed, trade resumed and markets began to flourish. At the time, the Burmese did not have coined money and used bullion, although the Indian silver rupee was accepted in the coastal regions. One observer commented that a "silver tickal, or dinga, is nearly the weight of a Madras rupee; and before the war broke out, one hundred seers, or about two hundred pounds of rice could be purchased for a tickal: the price, however, during my visit [in 1825], was thirty. Every shopkeeper has a small box, containing scales to weigh the bullion given in payment for commodities; the weights are modelled after the figure of griffons, cows, etc., The inferior currency is lead, with which fish, vegetable, tobacco are purchased".

The writer, Alexander, commenting on the Burmese, said that most of the men were athletic, and that the average height was about five feet eight inches. However, he found that the women were on the small side, but well-formed. He noted that the working people were extremely abusive, and when they "challenge one another to fight, they strike their left arm at the elbow with the right hand, exclaiming, "youk ya!" [*yauk kyar*], or "here's a proper man for you!" He also observed that the people were "exceedingly fond of music and poetry. They have bands of music, consisting of circles of gongs, drums and pieces of bamboo of different lengths fixed on strings, which being struck with a short stick, produce a sound resembling that of a piano. Their dancing consists of turning round slowly on one spot, and gracefully moving the arms and hands in circles".

According to Alexander, despite the troubled times the dockyards of Yangon were busy; in particular he mentions a large frigate of thirty-six-guns which was being built for the Imam of

"Old Monastic House - A
Road in Rangoon" by
Colesworthy Grant, 1855.

... the Wungyi Maong-kaing [Maung Khaing, the Governor] was reputed to be for a Burman, a man of humanity; yet, notwithstanding, he had committed his full share of cruelty since the announcement of the insurrection. In the first action which was fought, three Talaing [Mon] were killed, and one prisoner made; the heads of the first were struck off, and, to make the number even, that of the prisoner also; these heads were carried in triumph through the town. The Burman warriors displayed their courage by running up to them and wounding them with their spears....some Talaings were seized in the town, under suspicion of attempting to set fire to it. They and their families, including women and children, were buried alive, by being thrown into a well and covered over with earth. The person to whom the immediate execution of this atrocity was consigned, was the Sad'hauwun [Sar-daw Wun] or steward of the [royal] household.

CRAWFURD, 1829.

The richly gilded Rath or royal carriage captured at Tavoy in 1824. It was decorated with 20,000 gems and was later exhibited at the Egyptian Hall, Piccadilly, London, in 1825. *The Mirror,* **December 10 1825.**

၁၈၂၄ခုနှစ်တွင် အင်္ဂလိပ်များ ထားဝယ်မှ လန်ဒန်မြို့သို့ သယ်ယူသွား သော စစ်ကိုင်း မင်း ၏ တသိမ် တန် ရွှေရထား တော်ကြီး

Muscat and named *The Bandoolah*, after the celebrated, but recently deceased Burmese general; a curious choice of name for an Islamic vessel. Between 1786 and 1824, 111 vessels of between 800 and 1000 tons were built in the local dockyards.

Possibly the earliest scenes of the town and its environs to be published in the West appeared in Joseph Moore's lavishly produced *Eighteen Views Taken at and near Rangoon in 1825*. The album consisted of aquatints which only included small areas of the heavily stockaded town, and several views in and around the Shwedagon Pagoda. Nevertheless, the collection is a superb visual documentation of the first war between the British and the Burmese. For other pictorial records of the period, which are invaluable, we are indebted to some of the British military personnel. Judging by the numerous watercolours and sketches which have survived, many spent their spare time making full use of their talents by recording the scenes around them.

The British Army finally left on December 9 1826, after formally handing back the region, and having invited the new Burmese Governor and his suite to a banquet. On their departure from the port a salute of nineteen guns was fired, and the Burmese flag was hoisted over the King's Wharf. In town, the occasion was celebrated with music and dancing.

The festivities, however, were short lived. In 1827 Mon nationalists, under the able leadership of the Governor of Syriam, Smin Bawor (his Burmese name was Maung Sat) seized Dalla, and destroyed Kemmindine. He was aided by the Karens, who had also been persecuted by the Burmese for centuries, and consequently were of a passive nature, but had now decided to throw in their lot with the Mon. Sitke Maung Htaw Lay (1776-1869) Governor of Dalla, who was also a Mon, was not prepared to fight Smin Bawor, and afraid of being implicated in the uprising and executed by the Burmese he prudently fled with his people, numbering nearly 2,000, to British held Moulmein.

Smin Bawor, who was of royal blood, was so confident of success that he declared himself king. His people had been misled earlier by Sir Archibald Campbell into thinking that should they place themselves under the protection of the British, there was a possibility that their

kingdom would be restored. Now that the Burmese were once again in control in Lower Burma, and out for revenge, the Mon had no alternative but to make a last desperate stand.

Tatkalay, with its Chinese quarter, was taken by the Mon, but was recaptured by the Burmese Governor who placed a reward of thirty ticals on the head of every Mon rebel. When order was finally restored in town, Mon civilians who were unfortunate enough to fall into Burmese hands were put into bamboo cages and burnt with their families. For Smin Bawor, and thousands of his race, safety lay in British held Tenasserim. Thus began the last great migration of the Mon from their ancient homeland of Ramannadesa.

Meanwhile, suspicion was cast on the Chinese of Tatkalay and they were accused of collaborating with the Mon; their punishment was to be sold as slaves. Alexander said that at the time a considerable part of the population was "composed of Chinese or Fokis [Fukien] (as they term themselves), who are merchants, shopkeepers, artisans, and constitute the most industrious portion of the inhabitants". For a 'celestial' to be sold as a slave was a degrading situation, and when the terrible news reached China and the Malacca Straits, Chinese junks avoided the area for some time. Yangon was utterly in ruins and for a while commerce ceased. Despite this

"Yangon the principal port of the Birman Empire". An exaggerated view of the town, showing the teak stockade and the principal pagodas. To the left is the Shwedagon, and on the right is the Botataung Pagoda, one of the few shrines to have survived the British demolition teams in the early 1850s. *The Illustrated London News, December 6, 1845.*

ရန်ကုန်မြစ်နှင့်သစ်တပ်များ ဝိုင်း ထားသောမြို့ရွှေခင်း

devastation an enthusiastic attempt was made by the Governor to collect arms from the various foreign dealers who now appeared in town. He was so successful that by the end of 1827, when an Armenian ship loaded with guns for sale arrived, it was turned away.

The first panoramic view of the port of Yangon only appeared in 1831, when James Kershaw's sketch was included in *Views in the Burman Empire*. The somewhat picturesque scene depicted an immensely long stockade, thickly wooded hills, and huge towering shrines; the trend among British artists of this period was to distort the height of pagodas, and make them look larger then they really were. Between the defences and the river stretched a long line of wooden houses built on piles. The sketch also included one of the principal gates called the Yodayar Dagar (The Ayutthaya Gate) with its twin pavilions; this was situated close to the Botataung Pagoda. It was an idyllic and busy scene which gave no indication of the fear-ridden and precarious conditions in which the inhabitants lived under the all powerful Governor.

In 1841 Yangon was favoured by the presence of Tharrawaddy Min (r.1837-46) who, accompanied by his court, decided to come on a pilgrimage to the Shwedagon; this was to be the last visit by a reigning monarch. Amidst great celebrations he had the *stupa* regilded, and ordered a huge bell to be called the Mahatisadda Ghanta, for the pagoda. Having heard that the British fleet had proceeded up the river with ease to attack the town, he made plans to build a new administrative centre further inland, and named it Aung-myai-aung-hnin (victorious city); it was known locally as Okklapa, after a legendary kingdom which was claimed to have existed in the area.

Demolition of the old town and the dilapidated stockade commenced, and only the main defences along the waterfront were retained; work proceeded at a slow pace. His courtiers, however, possibly becoming aware of his deteriorating mental condition, persuaded the king to return to his capital Amarapura. By 1845, "he had become so outrageous that scarcely any one dared to go near him". During one of his attacks, the king speared to death Maung Youk Gyi, the former Governor of Rangoon. It was rumoured that as his condition deteriorated rapidly, the party in power had him secretly put to death in 1846. At the new town he founded the defences had still not been completed. The decrepit condition into which the area along the river front had fallen can best be judged in Colesworthy Grant's *Rough Pencillings of a Rough Trip to Rangoon,* in 1846, which is now in the Oriental and India Office Collections of the British Library.

Tharrawaddy Min's son, Pagan Min (r.1846-53), began his reign well but was easily seduced into a life of dissipation and animal sports, while his incompetent favourites effectively ruled the kingdom. Despite the disastrous war of 1824, the Burmese court was still insular, and arrogantly naive in deluding itself of its supposed superiority over all races. It chose to ignore the outside world, and felt that it could match the military might of any of the leading powers. Although there were well-informed personalities in the administration, they prudently kept their heads down, as they were liable to be accused of being in the pay of foreigners - an extremely serious charge and one which could merit a painful death for the entire household.

The port of Yangon certainly had its share of autocratic Governors; one in particular, called Maung Oak, was an avaricious character with a weakness for young women. Despite having acquired about thirty concubines, no pretty maid was safe from him. If the parents of one refused to comply with his wishes, he would imprison them on the most trivial charges; their freedom was only gained when the girl was delivered up to him.

Maung Oak also claimed to be 'pious', and during his tenure was notorious for extorting money for the purpose of building a pagoda. One source claimed that his ruthlessly energetic efforts for the culmination of this project was one of the factors which indirectly triggered off the second clash with the British. As can be imagined, he was thoroughly disliked by the inhabitants who are said to have disrespectfully used his personal name when referring to him, rather than his official title as was the custom.

According to Emily, the second wife of Judson, the American missionary, the Deputy Governor in 1847 was even worse, and was described as a "most ferocious, bloodthirsty monster". She said that the courtyard of his official residence "resounded day and night with the screams of the people under torture" and that corruption, extortion, and intimidation were rampant. People were encouraged to inform on their neighbours, wife against husband, and child against parents. The victim was then dragged off to the local jail and tortured, and was not released until a heavy fine had been paid.

In 1851, incidents between the Governor and the British merchants increased. It was discovered that among the latter there were those who were smuggling and evading custom dues. One such character who was detested by the Burmese and who was known to be a spy was the disreputable Englishman, May Flower Crisp. He appears to have gone out of his way to cause trouble between the two Governments. On learning that hostilities were about to break out, Crisp sold a ship-load of arms to the Burmese, and when payment was not forthcoming demanded compensation from the Governor General in Calcutta!

Recently published material for this period indicates that the British, in particular the arrogant Commodore Lamberts acted in a high-handed manner, and were determined to humiliate the Burmese court. Lambert was described as having a 'combustible' personality totally unsuited for this particularly sensitive operation. He was also unfortunate in having officers who were prejudiced against the Burmese and who deliberately provided misleading advice which was not conducive to peace.

During the second half of 1851, two incidents involving the Burmese Governor and the Captains of the *Monarch* and the *Champion* came to a head. This was to lead to the sudden appearance of the formidable Lambert on November 25, accompanied by two warships - the Second Anglo-Burmese War was about to begin.

Although an anxious Maung Oak did all he could to defuse the situation, a terse letter from the President-in-Council reminding Pagan Min of the earlier treaty was forwarded by Lambert to Amarapura. One of the items insisted on the recall of Maung Oak. A civil, but evasive, reply was received by the British, and Maung Oak was replaced by U Hmone on January 4 1852. Lambert, however, instantly suspected the intentions of the new incumbent, as he arrived with thirty thousand men. Intelligence also reached him that new Governors, each accompanied by large number of troops, had also been sent to Bassein and Martaban.

The tense situation escalated further, due to misunderstandings between both parties. One of the villains in this piece being a Captain Latter, an interpreter of the Bengal Native Infantry, who appeared to have been intent on starting a war. He deliberately made mischief between the hot-headed Lambert and the newly arrived but inexperienced Governor who is said to have been of a naive and peaceful disposition. In one incident, Latter and a companion appeared at the Governor's residence in a drunken state and were offensive, but then reported back to Lambert that they had been ignored and badly treated.

Lambert immediately ordered the three main rivers of the Delta to be blockaded with the aid

I have been on shore, and have visited the Great Pagoda. I was much struck with the Dagon, which is a mass of brick and stones, cased over and gilt, and rising about 250 or 300 feet: it is surrounded by small pagodas and elaborately carved houses, containing multitudes of gilt and marble images, great bells, etc., The base is surrounded by guardian winged monsters like griffons, their wings inlaid with coloured glass, and gilt in strange barbaric taste. I have got all sorts of curiosities in the shape of images and little gilt gods; also a sword and gilt hat, which a chief left in the trenches; and a collar, not of much value, which I got off the stockade the first morning I landed. The destruction in the town amongst the houses was very great: the native troops destroyed everything in the way of furniture that they could not carry off; and I pitied the poor Rangoon people, who, I believe, are rather favourable to us than otherwise. The town was defended by picked men down from the capital, Ava [Amarapura]; they wore red uniforms, and gilt hats.

The burning of the stockades and shelling the pagodas on the night of Easter Monday was a scene of havoc. The troops were landed in the morning, and had some sharp skirmishing, in which several were killed and wounded: so it was determined to clear out the stockades between the pagoda and the shore by heavy fire from the ships, and thus create a diversion. We set fire to the stockades commanding the river; the rest of the fires were occasioned by red-hot shot and shell, and carosses, which we poured into the inland stockades. I soon witnessed an illumination such as I had never seen before: the thunder of the heavy guns, and the rush and explosion of shell and rockets was indescribably grand; while the great Dagon pagoda, gilt from summit to base, shone out occasionally with a lurid light reflected on it in the background. There were fourteen ships of war employed in this affair of Rangoon.

It was a horrid sight visiting the stockades the morning after the fire: poor wretches, dead, and some wounded (but most of the latter had been carted off), were laying about, and the dogs tearing them to pieces, with crows and vultures gorging themselves till they could scarcely fly. In the magazine that we blew up, some of the dead had been so burnt as to fall to pieces when touched. The effect of our fire was fearful: indeed, nothing could have stood such heavy guns. But the Burmese fought with spirit till completely driven out.

THE ILLUSTRATED LONDON NEWS, JUNE 26, 1852.

Above: View from the Signal Pagoda showing part of the cantonment and the Royal Lakes in the distance. Bourne and Shepherd. c.1870s. ရခုအလံပြဘုရာ ဟုခေါ် နေကြသော မင် လက်ဝဲဘုရာ ပေါ်မှရှုခင် ၊ ၁၈၇၀ခုနှစ်လောက်တွင် ရိုက်ကူ ထာ သည်

Left: A Burman soldier of the lower ranks. *The Illustrated London News*, August 21 1852. ဒုတိယအင်္ဂလိပ် မြန်မါစစ်ပွဲတွင်ရဲစွမ် သတ္တိရှိရှိနှင့်ပြည်ပမှအဖွန္တရယ်ကိုခုခဲ့သောမြန်မာစစ် သာ

of newly arrived warships. British subjects were then hurriedly taken on board the vessels for safety. Although Lambert had been warned by Lord Dalhousie not to provoke any hostilities, he imperiously seized Pagan Min's man-of-war, the *Yenanyin*. As the king's vessel was being defiantly towed away, the Burmese had no option but to retaliate with a cannonade from their batteries on shore. This was just what Lambert had been waiting for, and in the return of fire from the British warships which were equipped with the most destructive weapons of the day, the Burmese defences were silenced. Destroyed, too, were a large number of gilded war canoes and other private boats in the harbour.

In town all was pandemonium, with the inhabitants fleeing in their thousands to the safety of the thick jungle which ringed the port. Meanwhile, Lambert returned to Calcutta to report to the Governor General. When told of the news Dalhousie wrote wearily to a friend and said: "So that fat is in the fire".

A second ultimatum, worded in "haughty and imperative terms" by Dalhousie, was then received by the Burmese court. It was offensive in the extreme, demanding among other things that "Your Majesty will agree to pay, and pay at once, one million rupees in satisfaction of the claims of the two captains, and in compensation for the loss of property suffered by British merchants in Rangoon..." On receipt of this the court at Amarapura went into deep shock, for the "Lords of the Thunderbolt, under whose Golden Feet other rulers placed their heads in humble submission" had never before been addressed in this manner. Dalhousie stipulated that a reply, or action, was expected within fifteen days. None came. The Burmese did not seek confrontation, but matters were now out of their control and there was now no turning back. Many felt that it was better to die fighting than become slaves of these 'foreign rebels'. War was declared by the British on April 1 1852.

U Hmone, the Governor, ordered the strengthening of the stockade of the new town built by Tharrawaddy Min. The defences took in the Shwedagon Hill, on the terrace of which were mounted 100 cannon. Unfortunately, the guns were all fixed facing south, as this was the direction from which the British were expected to attack. What remained of the central section of the old town by the riverside was dismantled or burnt, and some of the houses of the foreign merchants were looted by the royal troops. Only the dwellings outside the stockade were left intact. A strong palisade was also erected along the riverbank. The British were to marvel at the speed in which the huge logs could be put into place and at the way the Burmese could tunnel forward without exposing themselves to enemy fire.

As hostilities were about to commence, the British military authorities discovered that several of their officers had gone over to the enemy and were training them! One in particular was a Lieutenant Impey, who appears to have taken a liking to the Burmese, and no doubt felt appalled at the thought that they were being pitted against a disciplined and well equipped modern army. Earlier, in August 1851, the *Madras Athenaeum* had noted that Impey had once ordered "a hundred dozens of beer on the occasion of a Burmese Nautch [dance performance]. It ought to be a source of universal regret, that good tipple should have been consumed to such an extent by niggers who must have been unable to appreciate its value".

When battle commenced, although the Burmese put up a strong fight, a continuous bombardment from the British warships prevented them from advancing towards the river. A report which appeared in a Calcutta newspaper said that the "the Burmese fought like furies; the poor fellows had no alternative: their wives and children being held in security by their king for the fulfilment of their duty as fighting men".

Throughout the battle, fires raged in the various parts of the town and across the river at Dalla. The British, tipped off by May Flower Crisp's son about the eastern stairway of the Shwedagon which was not strongly defended, were able to seize the pagoda stockade on April 14. This put them in a powerful position directly behind the Burmese lines. Brave as they undoubtedly were, Pagan Min's army had no option but to retreat down the southern and western stairways into the jungle. Eye witnesses reported seeing numerous gold umbrellas of rank flashing in the sun, which their bearers tried unsuccessfully to hold over the heads of the rapidly departing commanders and officers.

The *Bengal Hurkaru* stated on May 7 that Impey was with the enemy and "had been at great pains in disciplining the Burmese soldiers, and that it was only owing to the superior training introduced by him that Jack Burmah has been able to fight so well". On hearing the news Impey's brother was so outraged that he is said to have offered five hundred rupees for his head! Impey was last seen riding off with his newfound friends, after the storming of the Shwedagon stockade; he finally escaped to Bangkok where he was employed to drill the royal troops. Another deserter was an officer called Harrison who had a boyish habit of leaving his name carved on tree trunks - to irritate the pursuing British soldiers.

The British had come fully prepared for this war, so that the chronic shortages of accommodation, food, and medicines experienced during the previous encounter with the Burmese in 1824 were not repeated. Provisions were plentiful, and all that was necessary for the building of sixty temporary barracks was produced by Chinese carpenters at Moulmein, and reassembled on site. The numerous monasteries clustered around the Shwedagon were also used as quarters for some of the regiments.

A Correspondent, writing for *The Illustrated London News* said that he found "the Rangooners generally much attached to the English, and expressed their desire to be placed under their rule, as they are aware of the advantages enjoyed by their brethren in the Tenasserim provinces, where they are beyond the tyranny of petty governors, and where their property and lives are equally protected with those of the English".

Other major towns which saw fierce fighting were Bassein, Prome and Pegu. In the outlying regions, the villages were to be plagued for many years by bands of *dah-pya* (sword flashers) a Burmese term for dacoits or armed thugs, many of whom had deserted from the royal army and whose mindless savagery and wanton cruelty struck terror in the hearts of their own people.

အင်္ဂလိပ်တို့ ရှင်္ရာမှုသစ်ဆန်း လာသောရန်ကုန်မြို့

From Pagoda to Godown

MAKING A NEW CITY

1852-71

The British had been confident of victory from the onset of the war, and had no intention of handing back Rangoon to the Burmese. By September 1852, plans for a new port and city had already been prepared. As the Burmese court could not bring itself to sign a treaty, Lord Dalhousie annexed the province of Pegu on December 20 1852, effectively turning Pagan Min's realm into a landlocked kingdom.

Despite its immediate drawbacks, such as the numerous creeks and low-lying marshy ground, the potential of the river-side site by the spectacular Shwedagon was recognised. The ancient fishing village of the Mon, which had seen so many changes over the centuries, was about to experience upheavals of an unprecedented magnitude, with hundreds of its old Buddhist landmarks being swept away for ever. Henceforth, the town was to become known officially as Rangoon, although the anglicized version was already being used by Symes as early as 1795, and appeared as such in maps from 1800 onwards. Dautrimer, in his *Burma Under British Rule* said that it was based on the Arakanese pronunciation of Yangon.

A map by Lieutenant Barnett Ford which showed Rangoon in April 1852, included the stockaded new town of Tharrawaddy Min, which enclosed an area to the south and west of the Shwedagon. Although the old abandoned town by the river is shown in ruins, it was still connected to the rest of the land by bridges; some of these had been demolished by the retreating Burmese army and had been reduced to seven.

Left: Detail of the Kyun-daw Monastery, near Myinegon.

Monasteries in Rangoon. The base of the hill on which the Shwedagon stands was once covered by numerous shrines and monasteries. Many were destroyed after the Second Anglo-Burmese War of 1852. The structure in the foreground has lost its roof ornaments, while the carvings on the building in the background have survived. c.early 1870s.

၁၈၇၀ခုနှစ်လောက်မှ အင်္ဂလိပ်အာနာရှင်များ ရန်ကုန်မြို့တွင်မြေရှင် ရာ ဖျက်ဆီ ခြင်
ခံရသော ဘုန် ကြီ ကျောင် များ လိုက်ရရှာသော ရှေ ခေတ်ဘုန် ကြီ ကျောင် များ

... as if by some magical power, a flourishing town, teeming with inhabitants all as busy as bees, has already risen on the ruins of Rangoon. Where one short month ago was to be seen nothing but the wreck and ruin which wait on 'glorious war', the marks of destruction and devastation caused by contending armies, with a solitary Pongyi's house [monastery] left standing here and there only to relieve the prevailing desolation of the scene, we now have a dense mass of habitations, with new ones springing up almost hourly in every direction, the bazaar extends a long way, full of shops and stalls, and these full with commodities and stores of all kinds, and no want of customers to buy them. The vendors are almost exclusively women, some young, and as pretty as I think it is possible for a Burmese beauty to be. It is a common custom for the Burmese women to preside at stalls in the public market places, while their worse halfs, fathers, brothers, sons are employed in some mechanical labour. By the way, a multitude of Burmese coolies and carpenters have found employment in our camp, and most willingly do they come in to earn their daily wages.

THE BOMBAY GAZETTE, JUNE 15 1852

The map, which is not as detailed as the one made in 1824 differs slightly from the latter, an example being the Sule Pagoda which is shown as being on an isolated island. It can only be assumed that at the time Ford was conducting his survey, the water level in the area had risen. The name of the premier landing stage, which was formerly known as the China Wharf, was changed to the King's Wharf. This important commercial area was situated to the west, and outside the protection of the old stockaded town.

The problems facing the British were enormous, one of the priorities being the immediate enforcement of law and order in Rangoon and its environs. In May 1852, Captain Latter and Lieutenant Ardagh were appointed military magistrates. A private letter which was published in *The Times of India* said that "the police of this place is an object of some interest just now owing perhaps to its inability to cope with the evil-doers. But the police has been rather on its mettle in consequence of a number of taverns having sprung up for the entertainment of Jack [British sailors]. The sailors, under the exciting influences of these public houses, usually betray a strong inclination for a row, and the police people have not the most distant chance of putting down the breaches of the peace that thus ensue. As for the tribe of robbers and thieves, the police has got pretty well used to them, and does not display any great solicitude on their account. Indeed, the plundering parties seem to have it all their own way". The antiquated port administration system under Burmese rule had to be replaced by one which was in use in India. For the time being an embargo was placed on the export of timber as it was needed for building purposes. Grain was also not allowed to be shipped abroad; this was to prevent a serious food shortage, as the Delta was still in an unsettled condition.

In town, gangs of labourers were organised to clear the enormous amount of debris, which was

Public Offices in the Strand. Building work began in the 1870s. Reclamation of land is still in progress in the foreground.

၁၈၇၀ခုနှစ်လောက်တွင်ရိုက်ကူ ထ ၁ သောအစိုး ရ ရုံ ကြီ များ

the result of the bombardment from the British warships. Along the river front, the huge teak posts which were used to form the outer stockade were pulled up and retrieved as valuable timber. Everything else was cleared, the only pagodas left standing were the Sule and the Botataung; the latter was known to the British as the White Pagoda, an indication that at the time it was not gilded but had been covered in whitewash.

Contemporary accounts indicate that the civilian population which had fled to the surrounding jungles when hostilities commenced began to return, but were not allowed to settle in the new town built by Tharrawaddy Min; this sector was set aside for the cantonment. Being enclosed by an extensive stockade and overlooking the town below, the military authorities prudently decided to take up residence within its protective defences whilst teams of coolies, reported as being 2,000 men and women, cleared the jungle on the selected sites. Though tents were in use for the time being, the construction of temporary barracks and houses for the officers was authorised. There was even accommodation for "the state-licenced harlots" who had been brought over from India. As the British army consolidated its position outside Rangoon and set up its cantonments, similar establishments were to be installed in such places as Akyab, Bassein, Thayetmyo and Toungoo.

Shrine within the Shwe-dagon complex, with images of the type looted and vandalised by the British forces.

... the personal superintendence of the Prize Agents, the idols are being broken open, excavated, I should say, with pick axes, as in some, treasure has been found. These idols are representations of female figures in a squatting posture, about ten feet high, the arms and face being white, and the drapery about the upper part of the head and the lower part of the body gilt; in one was found a roll of silver [possibly inscribed], and a bottle in which there were some small rubies. Europeans take to no work with better will than destroying anything. A number of the gods and goddesses present now a most wretched appearance, the valuables are generally deeply set in the region of the heart, and often in the head.

THE BENGAL HURKARU, JUNE 4 1852

In other parts of the town makeshift structures were soon springing up in the designated areas to accommodate the returning Burmese and the thousands of workers who were arriving from India to take advantage of the building boom. The way was being prepared for the gradual metamorphosis of the "dirty little town" into a great commercial city.

Captain Latter, the military magistrate, was also given the responsibiliy of Prize Agent, much against the wishes of the British soldiers. Latter appears to have had a sadistic streak, and in his role as guardian of law and order was quick to administer the cane, especially to non-Europeans. Understandably, he was hated by the Burmese, and British native troops alike. In Rangoon, the screams which were said to have emanated from the court house during the days of the Burmese Governor, were once again a familiar sound. As complaints against Latter began to pour in, *The Bengal Hurkaru* in September 1852 reported that Dalhousie had to step in and "put a check upon his rigorous proceedings in his capacity of Magistrate, especially in regard to corporal punishment, in which he so much delighted." Earlier, attempts had been made on Latter's life, and he was robbed of a large quantity of cash and clothes, which presumably did not improve his temper.

In the October of that year, the paper added that as there were fears of incendiaries, a Captain Simpson had given orders for the thatch and bamboo roofs of all the Government warehouses to be covered in mud. This inexpensive precaution worked so well that Captain Latter ordered all the house owners in the town to do likewise; despite protests, his order was put into practice.

The authorities were also to have trouble with the over zealous Latter in his capacity as the Prize Agent. It would seem that a Major Fraser, the Commanding Engineer, had been encouraged to reopen the tunnel which had been dug into the base of the Shwedagon in 1824, in search of treasure. His excuse was that he was testing to see whether the site would be suitable for a powder magazine. Fortunately, he was stopped. In Moulmein, Sitke Maung Htaw Lay, the ex-governor of Dalla, heard that the Shwedagon Pagoda was being broken into again by British soldiers and lodged a strong protest with the military authorities. Thanks to his efforts further damage was prevented.

Nevertheless, other prizes were more easily acquired by the British army. Among the impressive finds in a secret passage under the Shwedagon, was an iron chest with the contents of the ex-Governor's Treasury. *The Illustrated London News* stated that one of the trophies taken from the Shwedagon platform by the Madras Artillery was a large bronze bell which was estimated to be worth £17,000 (about rs.170,000); when it was cast, gold and silver ingots had been thrown in to the crucible. Looting of Buddhist shrines certainly took place, though the damage was not as serious as that perpetrated during the first war of 1824. *The Calcutta Englishman* reported that "the work of delving into every image in the place, of which there are many, was perseveringly carried out, but apparently not with the knowledge of the Prize Agents, as the European Artillery sold in great numbers the silver images and the bottles of rubies that were found inside".

Another strong protest was made, this time by Captain Arthur Phayre on his arrival in Rangoon to take up his new post of Commissioner of Pegu. Dalhousie immediately issued an order to prevent further vandalism of this most sacred of Buddhist shrines, and the thousands of pagodas throughout the province. Dalhousie said that the soldiers called the images 'Tommies', and confessed that he himself was guilty of secretly acquiring some during his first visit to the town in 1852.

The house of U Chin,
Kandawgyi Road.

70

For the British troops who were not on active service, boredom became a problem, for apart from military parades there was very little to do. The rainy season also put a stop to much of the fighting. One newspaper noted that a Book Club had been formed, with "an entrance fee of twenty rupees and a subscription of three rupees a month. The plan is to get out books and periodicals direct from England. The poorer sort of reading people here think the rates too high, and are endeavouring to organise a small club of their own, but their limited number and means would scarcely meet the object in view".

Others decided to organise entertainment by turning one of the more spacious *zayat*, or rest-houses on the Shwedagon into a theatre, and fitting it out with "excellent scenery". *The Calcutta Englishman* reported that on July 28 1852, the dramatic company in Rangoon gave their first performance, and that "the pieces were the *White Horses of the Peppers*, and *Circumstantial Evidence*, and were very creditably performed. The scenery was exceedingly well painted, the drop scene being a faithful representation of the storming of the Great Pagoda on the 14th April". Several other companies were also formed to entertain the troops. However on the night of November 1 1852, a magazine nearby blew up, killing some men; destroyed, too, was Rangoon's very first Western-style theatre, which caught fire.

The plans for the new city proceeded at an energetic pace, with much enthusiasm being exhibited by those taking part. It was to be built on a strip of land about four miles wide, which was bordered on the east by the Pazundaung Creek, and on the south and west by the Hlaing (Rangoon) River. At the time, there was a Dr Montgomerie who had been involved in the creation of the city of Singapore who felt himself qualified to offer his services to the planning committee.

Montgomerie, who was later to be honoured by having a main street named after him, submitted his ideas in September 1852, for a commercial city of a chess-board design, which would leave an open space or strand along the river bank. The streets were to be sixty feet wide, with wells at every 100 feet. There were to be drains, an efficient sewage system, and trees planted to provide shade. Some of these suggestions were followed in part by a Lieutenant Alexander Fraser, a young Scot from the Bengal Engineers, who was ultimately responsible for planning the city.

The amount of construction work involved was formidable. One of the priorities was to arrest the erosion of the river bank and prevent the flooding of large areas of land at high tide. This was done by sinking along the strand the huge teak logs retrieved from the dismantled stockades, and by raising the height of the barrier by several feet. As central Rangoon was low-lying, tons of earth from the outskirts were carried in by carts to a point from which it was conveyed to the various parts of the town. There, coolies and other carters distributed the material to the required sites. In many areas, the level of the surface also had to be raised; in one large sector alone over four million cubic feet of earth was used. It was observed that for a time, the area between the river and the Shwedagon resembled a large plain, as smooth as a "military parade ground".

As outbreaks of fire were frequent in the scorchingly hot dry season, it was wisely decreed that only brick buildings would be allowed in the central commercial area, and that the use of wood and thatch should be avoided. Public works which involved construction and reclamation were to be funded by the sale of land which was to be disposed of in blocks. Needless to say, alterations to the original plans were made by Fraser as work progressed. But despite his sterling efforts there were many who were critical of his final layout of the city.

When the principal streets came to be named, Dalhousie insisted that they be called after some of the leading personalities who were involved in the last war. His choice, which smacked of favouritism, caused much resentment in some quarters; one of the streets bore the name of the unpopular Captain Latter. Another, named after Sir Arthur Phayre, the first Chief Commissioner, originally presented a stunning sight, as it consisted of a long avenue bordered by whitewashed and gilded pagodas leading in the direction of the Shwedagon; these ancient shrines were later all razed to the ground. The pious and capable Sitke Maung Htaw Lay, who had earlier been made a magistrate at Moulmein and who had assisted the British, was not forgotten; the street named after him is the only one to have survived into modern times; all the others have now had their names changed. Whilst wooden posts for street lighting were erected, it was noted that the oil lamps appeared only in some of the more important areas; the entire town had to wait for this facility until 1875. Once darkness had fallen, it was still the custom among the majority of the inhabitants to secure the front door. People rarely ventured out at night unless it was on an important errand. Social calls were usually conducted during daylight hours. Those who were abroad at night were mainly Europeans, who either travelled in carriages with lights, or if on foot, were proceeded by a servant carrying a lantern.

As construction work progressed in the central sector, the temporary huts of the squatters had to be dismantled, which caused a considerable amount of disquiet, as the people, many of whom were manual labourers were relocated to outlying areas; public transport had still to be organised. The reluctance to move was understandable as most of the activities were in town and on the waterfront, where new structures and wharfs were being constructed. Meanwhile, along the river,

"A Prize-fight in Burmah". A scene on the Shwedagon terrace which took place between the Rangoon Pet and the Moulmein Slasher. *The Illustrated London News*, September 23 1876.

၁၈၇၆ခုနှစ် ရွှေတိဂုံဘုရားပေါ်မှ လက်ဝှေ့ပွဲ

Right: A delicately carved monastery. Buildings on this small scale were used more for ceremonial occasions, and housed only a few resident monks. c.1870s.

ပန် ပုလက်ရာအထူ ကောင် လှသော၁၈၇၀ခုနှစ်လောက်မှဘုန် ကြီ ကျောင်

Ngme Sein and Ngwe Yi.

A Burmese *lun-pwe* (tug of war) usually performed during times of drought. The rain spirit was believed to enjoy riding in the middle of the rope, and later rewarded the people with much needed showers. *The Graphic*, January 4 1879.

၁၈၇၉ခုနှစ်မှ လွန်ပွဲ

the numerous little creeks were filled in and the bund strengthened. Fraser also decided to encircle the town with a wide canal, and although sections were dug the plan was eventually abandoned as being not viable; Canal Street survives as a memory of this project.

With the redistribution of sites, the leaders of the numerous religious communities were consulted and large plots handed over for the construction of churches, mosques, Chinese and Hindu temples, and a Synagogue. The enclosures in which hundreds of small pagodas and monasteries had once stood, and which had been demolished were callously taken over for secular use. None of these shrines or religious buildings were allowed to be repaired or rebuilt by the Burmese; it should be noted that once consecrated, such grounds are believed to be sacred in perpetuity, and that misfortune and poltergeist activities will afflict those foolish enough to live there.

In the central sector, markets on a more permanent scale were organised, and in some quarters it was noticed that street stalls had already begun to appear as early as May 1852, while fighting was still in progress. Some wealthy members of the Surati community decided to invest in Rangoon's first official market which they called the Surati Bazaar. The complex consisted of rows of connected sheds with narrow passages, in which the booths were crowded and posed a fire hazard. Lighting was bad, and due to lack of ventilation the smells were said to have been overpowering. For the British, the only establishment which catered to their needs was a large bamboo and thatch building owned by Messrs. Jordan & Co.

Newspapers from India were now readily available in Rangoon; a Mr. Lewis, the owner of the *Maulmein Chronicle* (1840) began producing the *Rangoon Chronicle* in 1853; it was published every Wednesday and Saturday. The paper was to pass through several ownerships and a change

of name to the *Pegu Gazette,* but did not survive the competition from the Calcutta newspapers, and circulation finally ceased in 1858.

During the same month the fragile tranquillity of Rangoon was suddenly shattered when a badly organised attempt to take the Shwedagon was made by Burmese patriots. Their aim was to capture the arsenal and the city, and massacre the British. Fortunately for the British the plans were leaked to the authorities who were able to move troops to strategic positions. On observing this, those involved lost their nerve and the ringleaders were arrested. In view of this incident, although the main platform and the north, east, and south stairways of the Shwedagon were handed back to the Pagoda Trustees, the western side of the hill was strongly fortified and taken over by the military authorities.

The year 1853 was to close with a particularly nasty and bizarre murder, which became the topic of conversation in Rangoon for some time. It was learned that the detested Captain Latter, who had been promoted to the rank of Deputy Commissioner of Prome, had been found brutally stabbed to death in his bed. After the frenzied attack his murderer had calmly draped a cheap *htamein* (woman's lower garment) over the corpse; according to Burmese tradition, such a degrading gesture carried out on a male was the ultimate insult.

As the military presence was noticeably strong in Rangoon, it led to the town being used as a dumping ground for some of the political prisoners connected with the Indian Mutiny. Among the internees held in the cantonment was Abu Zafar Bahadur Shah II, the last of the Mogul Emperors, who was an unwilling participant in the massacre of Englishmen and women in India. The aged ex-ruler survived until 1862, and was buried near the Shwedagon where his tomb can still be seen. His family was made to vacate the house assigned to them in the cantonment, and

An early teak house on
Taw-win Road, Ahlone.

... *came off the evening before last with much éclat. It was held in a very fine house that Dr McLelland had nearly completed outside the stockade. The strength of the floor was well tested by the circumstance that ten couples dancing at once did not cause the least vibration. The house is a fair specimen of what houses may be made of the magnificent wood of this country. The floors, walls, and ceiling are all teak, and remind one of the oak panelled chambers of ancestral halls of good old England. The rooms are large and airy, and the view commanded from it of the beautiful lake lying below, with the long sea of the tops of the green trees beyond, and a glimpse of the Irrawaddy, is charming.*

To those who have not seen a lady's face for more than a year and three quarters, the sight of a dozen well dressed and really very good looking English gentlewomen was a great treat. To enjoy a Polka with them was something even more. Dancing commenced at nine, and the doors were thrown open at twelve for supper, and a very good one it was, a great deal better than one generally sees on such occasions in India. The Champagne was excellent and abundant, and the dancing was resumed with increased vigour after supper till half past two o'clock. All Rangoon was there except the Editor of the Rangoon Chronicle [an unpleasant man who was not invited].

THE CALCUTTA ENGLISHMAN
ON RANGOON'S FIRST BALL, NOVEMBER 10, 1853.

were allocated a small building by the Surati Bazaar where they lived in poverty ignored by their fellow Muslims. One of the Princes of Delhi was later given a house opposite the Rangoon Jail, where he could be seen most days in the grounds, lying on his couch under the influence of drugs.

Another prisoner who planned the destruction of the Raj was Ram Singh, chief of the Kookhies, whose captured followers were dispatched by the British by being blown from cannon. A fanatic, Ram Singh was considered extremely dangerous and had to be guarded round the clock by four soldiers.

A less menacing exile was U Kyan Gyi, the son of the legendary General Maha Bandula. His father's title had been conferred on him by Pagan Min during the Second Anglo-Burmese War of 1852, and he had been sent down from Amarapura to drive the British out of the country. The new General soon became aware of the superior strength of the invaders, and for his subsequent failure to stop the British, his entire household at Amarapura was slaughtered by the king. U Kyan Gyi prudently surrendered to the British and was confined to Rangoon. He was still alive in 1855, and had his portrait painted by the English artist Colesworthy Grant.

Within the new city the sale of land progressed so well that most of the blocks in the commercial sector were sold. However, the new owners were slow to erect new buildings, speculating that their plots could be re-sold at a profit. As a result, the only substantial structures in Rangoon were the beautifully carved and gilded Buddhist monasteries, some of which were still occupied by the British administrators such as the District Commissioner, the Magistrate's Court and the Treasury. Other government officials had to sleep on board their vessels until suitable accommodation could be built for them.

The pressure on the construction industry was intense, with some people in this particular profession making fortunes. Gone were the flimsy mat structures of earlier years, and in their place rose substantial wooden houses. These were comfortable and airy, with wide verandahs and many windows, a design which was considered ideal for the tropics.

Map of Rangoon, 1897.

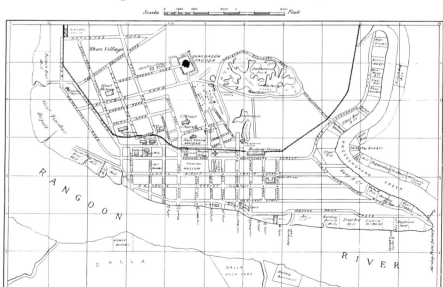

79

" Allandale." Rangoon.

As the civil administration began to take over, various civic departments were established. A postal system was also introduced to facilitate communications, and the son of the notorious May Flower Crisp was appointed Postmaster; this was said to have been his reward for his assistance in the storming of the Shwedagon stockade in 1852.

The question of sanitation now posed a problem. For some time the river had been used to dispose of the town's domestic waste, but now it was decided to have it removed in carts to the deep ravines on the outskirts. As a sewage system did not exist, each house was provided with a cesspit, but with a notable increase in population this method began to pose a health problem; wells became contaminated and deaths from mysterious illnesses increased.

Incidents of robbery also began to be reported. These were mainly the exploits of the dacoits (armed thugs) who preyed on the non-Europeans living in the outskirts of the town. This was a serious and continuing problem for the authorities.

For the British, in their roomy villas set within spacious gardens, life was made bearable only with the aid of their well-trained Indian servants. Entertainments were few, and although there were numerous opportunities to witness Burmese theatrical performances, the cultural and language divide was too wide to be crossed. Apart from a few outgoing personalities, Englishmen and women of the period did not think it proper for the ruling race to be seen consorting with non-Europeans.

By 1854, the need for a place of recreation for the British had became apparent, and so a barn-like structure of wood, with a thatch roof held down by a trellis of bamboos was built and called the Assembly Rooms. This had a wide covered verandah around three sides, each with its own stair. The interior, however, was quite opulent, with chandeliers hanging from the rafters, and ornamental lamps on the walls; large windows with glass panes admitted light during the day. Prints decorated the walls of the rooms which were furnished with tables and sofas. A billiard-room and a small library were also provided for its patrons; in the latter, almost all the illustrated papers from England were available, albeit out of date.

With an increasing number of English ladies arriving to join their spouses, a select Rangoon society began to emerge. Those who were fortunate to be admitted to this circle were bound by the rituals, unspoken rules and prejudices which had been imported direct from British India.

During the demolition of the numerous ruined Buddhist shrines many treasures of archaeological interest were discovered in the relic chambers. One such find, in April 1855, was under a pagoda on the eastern terrace of the Shwedagon and included solid gold vessels which are now believed to have belonged to the Mon Queen Bana Thau (r.1453-72).

Lord Dalhousie, who was interested in the find said that it was worth "about 25,000 rupees. A golden scroll which was with them bore an inscription which showed that the pagoda was built and the things buried by a queen about 500 years ago." The discovery was subsequently published in the *Journal of the Royal Asiatic Society* in 1857, thus preventing the hoard from being broken up and dispersed. The remains of this remarkable group of gold objects, representing Mon craftsmanship at its finest, are now conserved in the Victoria and Albert Museum in London. Other objects of precious metals were not so fortunate, one dare not think of the large number of historically important artifacts which have now been lost.

Dalhousie also took a keen interest in the development of Rangoon and paid it several visits. His last one was in 1855, when he expressed delight with the progress of the capital and predicted that it could become one of the more attractive cities of India. Under the organisation of Sitke Maung Htaw Lay regilding work was in progress on the Shwedagon, and Dalhousie donated 250 rupees towards the cost - a charitable act which delighted the Burmese. Before his death in 1869, Sitke Maung Htaw Lay also made repairs to the Naungdawgyi and the Sule pagodas.

Dalhousie was deeply impressed by the beautiful scenery toward the north of the town and suggested that the area be preserved and used as a park, with a drive encircling it. Despite plans being drawn up, it was not fully carried out, and the acres of rolling ground continued to be a jungle infested with snakes. Soon, though, squatters began to encroach on this precious space; it was even used by some Chinese farmers for their market gardens.

In town, fires in 1855 and 1857 caused devastation and undid all the work that had been done. Although thatch was forbidden to be used, the rule was not enforced; many of the fires started in buildings roofed with this material.

For the citizens of Rangoon one of the few public entertainments of the time were the races in which Shan ponies were used, and which were occasionally held on the parade ground belonging to the military. These animals which had been brought from the regions between China and the Shan States could be inspected and bought at a large village on the outskirts of the city where they were kept tethered to posts in long bamboo sheds.

"Elephant Steeplechase at Rangoon," which was held on the military parade ground. Shwedagon Pagoda in the background.
The Illustrated London News, September 25 1858.

ရနှစ်တွင်ရန်ကုန်မြို့မှာကျင်ပခဲ့သော ဆင်ပြိုင်ပွဲ

The Illustrated London News for September 25 1858, depicted a curious scene showing an elephant steeplechase. On this particular occasion there were thirteen elephants answering to names such as Delhi Bully, Shuffling Jimmy, and Ponderous Polly; each animal was ridden by its mahout and a British officer. A young male elephant called Soorul Jamal came in first, while poor Ponderous Polly did not quite make it.

Rangoon continued to grow. Henry Gouger, who had been a prisoner of the Burmese during the First Anglo-Burmese War of 1824, said that the town which not so long ago was a "den of extortion and robbery, has been transformed into a valuable seaport for commerce". Marshall, writing in the late 1850s, added that "where a dreary, boggy waste of ground once existed, now arose a row of palatial edifices on the strand, with an excellent broad roadway on the water-side, extending fully a mile". The task of reclaiming the land in the central part of the city had ceased by the early 1860s, whilst similar and much needed work in the north-eastern sector was not followed up. This meant that thousands of the poorer inhabitants, mainly Burmese and Indians, were still living in squalid conditions in huts built over marshy ground. Another health hazard were the market gardens owned by the Chinese, who used night soil as a fertiliser. As complaints increased, a Government order was issued to the proprietors which effectively forced the gardeners further out into the countryside.

Sanitation continued to pose a serious problem, but the lack of municipal funds held up the installation of a more satisfactory system for some time. Judging by the furious complaints in the local papers, the refuse collection system also appeared to have broken down frequently. Rubbish and dead animals were often seen on the roadside and were not removed for days. It is not surprising that Rangoon experienced many outbreaks of cholera, dysentery, plague, small-pox, and typhoid, resulting in high mortality rates.

It would seem that such deadly visitations were usually confined to the native quarters and rarely appeared in the healthier conditions of the cantonment. The other areas where the British mercantile community resided also seem to have been spared. It may have been that unlike the Orientals, Europeans were better informed about health matters and took precautions.

Despite these recurring outbreaks, which were virulent but fortunately brief, the commercial success of the city continued to grow. The epidemics which were fully reported in the papers of the day do not appear to have deterred foreign investors from setting up business in Rangoon.

Sailing ships were now providing a regular service between the United Kingdom and Burma. This involved an often extremely uncomfortable trip around the Cape of Good Hope. So little was known about the country that, until the 1880s, a large majority of people who were posted there approached its shores with a certain amount of trepidation. This was in part caused by some of the misinformed British residents of India who spread unfounded and uncomplimentary rumours about the "terribly unhealthy" climate, and the "savagery" of the natives.

On arrival in Rangoon, however, many of the newcomers were struck by the picturesque exotic sights and the friendliness of the Burmese. Those with experience of India were also surprised at the differences in character and behaviour between the two races. Most importantly, the European residents, with whom contact was unavoidable, were friendly.

The new 'lord' of the city was the Chief Commissioner, a post which was created in 1862, when the independently governed provinces of Arakan, Pegu, and Tenasserim were merged into the Province of British Burma. However, each region continued to be ruled by a Commissioner, who was answerable to the Chief Commissioner in Rangoon.

In independent Upper Burma, the subjects of Mindon Min (r.1853-78) soon heard of the settled conditions and opportunities available in British Burma. As a result, many migrating families braved the gauntlet of royal troops on the border to settle in areas which were being opened up. Other immigrants, who were encouraged by the British Government, arrived in their thousands from the Indian subcontinent. Used to the harsh conditions in their homeland, they were willing to work longer hours in the vast sweltering plains of the Delta. These virgin lands were being turned over to cultivation in order to produce more rice to satisfy the ever increasing demand.

The companies which prospered were those dealing either in timber or rice, but by the early

Burmese at Football, Rangoon

Left: The Town Hall, Immanuel Baptist Church, and part of Fytche Square, photographed from the terrace of the Sule Pagoda; at the time the wide platform of the Sule was free of small shrines. The single tramline in the road indicates that the picture was taken soon after the line had been extended by Messrs J W Darwood in 1885; this ran from China Street and along Dalhousie Street which can be seen in the picture.

၁၈၈၅ခုနစ်လောက်မှရန်ကုန်မြို့ တော်ခမ် မနှင့်ဘုရာ ရှစ်ခို ကျောင် ၊ ဆူ လောဘုရာ အတွင် မှရှိက်ကူ ထာ သည်

Above: a new architectural vocabulary for Rangoon.

General Post Office, Rangoon

Royal Hotel — Rangoon,

Gymkhana - Rangoon

Government House.

Race Stands, Rangoon

Chief Court - Burma.

1870s, the latter was to replace teak as the principal export of the province; the chief customers were Europe and India.

Although roads had been built to connect Rangoon with other towns, the principal form of transportation and communication was by water. Initially, a fleet of government-owned launches were maintained, but in 1865 it was decided to transfer the administration to a private company, later known as the Irrawaddy Flotilla Company. Under their competent management larger and well-designed steamers which were capable of carrying passengers and cargo were built at Dalla and provided an invaluable service for decades.

As the city began to expand, the construction and maintenance of roads caused a headache for the Public Works Department. Fluctuating funds were a recurrent problem. The ambitious planners of the city were also disappointed to see that while structures of timber were mushrooming, the erection of *pukka* (substantial brick) buildings in the private and business sectors was proceeding at a snail's pace.

Fortunately, during the early stages of the construction of the city, some of the more far-sighted administrators had designated the water-logged area on the south-eastern side of the Sule pagoda as a public garden and when funds became available work commenced with cart-loads of earth being spread over a considerable area to stabilise the ground. A section of one of the ponds was retained and its banks planted with trees. Originally known as Tank Square, further improvements were made between 1867-88, and the name was changed to Fytche Square, after the Chief Commissioner who succeeded Phayre in 1867. The park, with its exotic collection of trees and shrubs, became one of the more cherished places where people could congregate in the cool of the evening and listen to a military band which played from an ornate pavilion.

As the city became more settled, societies were formed and lectures and meetings held in one of the public halls. For some of the European residents interested in the flora of the country, annual shows for flowers, fruit, and vegetables were organised in the grounds of the Agri-Horticultural Society which had been founded in 1865.

In the field of education, it is known that although a Government School was already in existence by 1856, there were also privately run establishments. With an increasing number of Europeans bringing out their families, religious bodies, such as the Anglicans, Baptists, and Catholics, began opening schools of their own. Institutions such as St. Paul's School (1859), Anglican Diocesan Schools (1862), and St. John's College (1864) were to produce able administrators and workers for the various government departments. The pupils consisted of Europeans, Eurasians, Burmese, and others from the minority groups. Education took a further step forward when in 1866 a Department of Public Instruction was formed.

Among the civil servants, the role of the Town Magistrate appears to have been a difficult one, as he carried on his shoulders the burden of several departments. One in particular was the police force. Originally, the recruits who were under the supervision of European officers, were composed exclusively of tall fierce-looking men from Northern India. These men were not afraid to use their truncheons on trouble makers of any race, including some of the younger Buddhist priests who tended to prove troublesome at times. When Burmans came to be recruited, their racial identity was retained to a certain degree in their uniform. This consisted of a long sleeved jacket, a *gaungbaung* (turban) and a striped *pasoe* (sarong) which was tucked between the legs.

The Masonic Lodge, Rangoon. A large and spacious building built on brick pillars. Such houses were designed to catch the faintest breeze by having the living area on the first floor. c. 1870s.

၁၈၇၀ခုနှစ်လောက်မှအဆောက် အအုံနှင့်မြင် လှည် များ

Like their Indian counterparts, they, too, wore boots and were armed with either a thick stick, or sometimes a spear.

Curiously, the police force was underpaid. In 1867, the average wage for a police constable was between nine and eleven rupees per month, while some coolies could earn as much as fifteen. Although this was known, very little was done to improve the situation. This unfortunate state of affairs often left policemen open to temptation, forcing many to accept bribes, and to collude with the more hardened criminal elements. An increase in salary only came about in 1869, at the instigation of Fytche, the Chief Commissioner. Although a fresh attempt at recruitment brought in men of the right calibre, corrupting influences were always present, and a number of constables were continually having to be dismissed from the force.

Contemporary accounts suggest that the trouble spots in the city were located in the Burmese quarters of Kemmindine and Pazundaung, where criminal elements were known to reside, and where burglaries and robberies were being committed. Until 1858 the inhabitants had been allowed to retain arms, such as swords and guns, but in that year it was decided to confiscate them. The majority of law-abiding people surrendered their weapons, but others hid theirs and continued to prey on the community.

In the central commercial sector, once building work had been completed, the sale of land declined and further development by the authorities was held back because of financial difficulties. However, this was to change with the opening of the Suez Canal in 1869 which gave a further boost to the prosperity of Rangoon. Within a few years there was a dramatic increase in trade, as vessels no longer needed to use the dangerous Cape route, and steamships began replacing the old sailing clippers. With the increase in shipping in the Rangoon River, the need to reform fur-

A Dak Bungalow in the
jungle. c.1890s.

ရှေးရန်ကုန်မြို့တော်
ဂ္ဂလိုမြို့သို့တော

ther some of the port administration became apparent and accordingly the Strand Bank Committee was formed.

Another important step towards modernization was the formation of the Rangoon and Irrawaddy Valley State Railway. Although construction work began in 1869 the line which began at Rangoon and terminated at Prome, 161 miles away to the north, was not opened until 1877. In the area around Prome, much of the brick and stone work from the ancient Pyu city of Sri Kshetra (in Burmese Thayekhittaya) was used as foundation for the rail track; this vandalism was said to have been perpetrated by Indian contractors.

A sign of the increasing prosperity of Rangoon was signalled by the regilding of the Shwedagon in 1869. Earlier, it had been suggested to Mindon Min, by some of the Burmese in the city, that he should present a new finial for the pagoda. This was agreed to by the monarch, and one measuring thirty-three feet in height was constructed in seven sections. The entire iron base was lacquered and sheathed in pure gold. When assembled, a fifteen foot vane, ornamented with precious stones, some of which had been donated by the Buddhists of British Burma, was to be inserted at the top; the total value was variously estimated at between fifty and sixty thousand pounds. Although work was completed at Mandalay in 1870, the British made a request to the Burmese court to withhold the dispatch of the finial until the following year.

In 1871, the royal barge carrying the finial began a stately progress down the Irrawaddy accompanied by smaller vessels. Stops were made at the towns along the way. At each specially decorated landing stage, it was ecstatically welcomed by the pious who contributed yet more jewels. The moment the craft entered British territory a tight security screen was thrown around the vessel, and after an uneventful journey the little flotilla finally docked at Rangoon on October 22 1871.

A great multitude of people, predominantly Buddhists, lined the banks, many of them bowing down in the direction of the barge. Most of these pilgrims, among whom were entire families, had come for the occasion from the outlying districts. In the streets, the military and mounted police were out in force, and lined the route along which the valuable object passed. Enthusiastic volunteers carried the various parts of the finial on decorated carriages and palanquins, and finally up the steps of the sacred hill.

On the summit, a gigantic mesh-like bamboo scaffold had been erected around the Shwedagon, so that the dangerous work of assembling the *hti* (or finial) could be carried out in comparative safety. Unfortunately this joyous occasion was marred when, during an operation to hoist up one of the heavier sections, the taut ropes snapped, whipping three Shan scaffolders off their perch and down to their deaths hundreds of feet below.

Finally, the great moment came when the seven sections of the finial were screwed into place, and the bejewelled orb which terminated in a 'diamond bud' was fixed into place. When this was announced the entire platform which was seething with people erupted with shouts, songs, music and dancing. Among the Burmese, the occasion was considered to be one of the more memorable religious events of the nineteenth century, and in the history of their city. Much to the surprise of the British, throughout the ceremony, and during the celebrations which followed, the behaviour of the huge crowds was impeccable.

ရန်ကုန်မြို့၏ အခြေအနေ–၁၈၈၅ခုနှစ်အထိ

Prelude to War

CAPITAL OF LOWER BURMA
UNTIL 1885

The route followed by most ships from Madras to Rangoon was past the dangerous mile-long Alguada reef, where over the centuries, many a vessel had been wrecked. In 1861, the threat was neutralized with a 140 foot high lighthouse of granite masonry, the warning light from which could be seen for twenty miles. This was to be another brilliant achievement for Lieutenant Fraser who had earlier been responsible for the re-building of Rangoon; he was promoted to Captain.

As a ship approached the vast Irrawaddy delta, its passengers would have noticed the colour of the sea change from a blue-green to a muddy brown, glittering with sand particles brought down from the interior by innumerable creeks. Low-lying land with clumps of stunted trees would then have been sighted until the mouth of the Rangoon River was reached. The two-mile wide mouth of this artery was guarded by a pair of red obelisks, one on each bank, set up as a warning to the mariner. Large iron buoys also marked the edges of the numerous constantly shifting sandbanks. On entering the river the incoming vessel joined a variety of other craft which were either on their way to or leaving the port of Rangoon.

In the late 1860s, with the exception of certain prominent buildings on the Strand, much of the waterfront remained shrouded by a luxuriant curtain of trees, behind which rose a few church steeples, pagoda tops, and minarets. This medley of religious architecture was dominated by the huge Shwedagon.

In December 1874, Rangoon was visited by the Commander-in-Chief of the Madras Army Sir Frederick Haines and his wife. A municipal committee had taken over the administration of the city whereas previously

Left: Downtown Rangoon - corner of Phayre (Pansodan) and Fraser (Anawratha) streets.

this had been the responsibility of the Local Government. The visitors noted that on both banks of the river there were rice-mills, factories, warehouses, and wharfs - the most important being Godwin's Wharf - and the river itself was crowded with ocean-going ships, many being foreign vessels of all shapes and sizes, not to mention the often massive Burmese craft from upcountry with their distinctive appearance.

The Strand was now a broad macadamised street with imposing and substantial government offices, stores, and private houses; it was later to be extended for over two miles. Considering that Rangoon was a busy port, there was a shortage of better class hotels, and the three which enjoyed this distinction were invariably full. The first impression acquired of the city was that "abundance prevailed", and that the non-European inhabitants looked well fed and had a happy countenance. What an observer would not have known was that sanitation was still at a primitive level, and health hazards were numerous. But unlike other cities in the East, the roads were clean, and free of beggars. A lunatic asylum was established in 1870 and took the mentally ill off the streets.

In Burma, beggars tend to congregate along the long covered stairways that lead to pagodas knowing that here pilgrims cannot ignore their pitiful cries for alms. The Shwedagon, in particular, acted as a magnet to the blind, lame, and those ravaged by leprosy and other tropical diseases. Despite the opening of the General Hospital in a collection of wooden buildings in 1873, these 'professional' beggars avoided any attempt at medication.

Another group of social outcasts, known as *phayar-kyun* (pagoda slaves), could also be seen on the pagoda, selling offerings and other items. These were the descendants of people who had been dedicated to the shrine in the distant past, but who were still chained psychologically to their 'caste' by a hopeless sense of resignation and a blind following of tradition. It was said that although some pagoda slaves had been able to hide their origins and become successful business-men, many felt a compulsion to visit a shrine annually, and feed off the food offerings left by pil-grims. This was done secretly, and at the dead of night.

In Rangoon, an increasing number of streets were now lit by glass lanterns fed with kerosene oil, and in the cool season each orb of light attracted thousands of flying insects. These pests also in-vaded the houses, making life within extremely trying. Another anxiety, now confined to the

Burmese quarters, were the large number of feral dogs, which meant that rabies was a constant threat. The dreaded cry of *khway-yu* (mad dog) caused terrible panic and had the power to clear the streets instantly. The Surgeon General, CA Gordon, who was in Rangoon in 1874, visited these sectors and said that the mangy half-starved dogs swarmed everywhere. With typical British thoroughness, the Municipal authorities took action, and attempted to eradicate these strays twice a year with poisoned food. While this method had worked in the city and the cantonment, in the Burmese quarters many of the dogs were rushed indoors by the kind-hearted people whenever the official poisoners were sighted. Being Buddhist, they were very much against the taking of life - such notions of compassion seem quite contrary to the antics of marauding dacoits in the districts.

As the number of people in the city swelled, the central sector became overcrowded, and the system of providing each house with a cess-pit also had to be abandoned. The answer was to provide yet more carts to take away the night soil, but due to the lack of personnel who were prepared to do this type of work, it was not a success. Eventually, low-caste Indian sweepers had to be recruited from Calcutta and Madras. Unfortunately, the scheme with its compulsory tax proved so expensive that many households tried to evade it. The sweepers also realised that they were indispensable and often went on strike for higher wages, causing considerable inconvenience to the inhabitants.

The necessity of obtaining clean water for the growing city also became paramount, and several proposals were put forward. As a temporary measure it was decided to make use of the Royal Lakes. Permission was also obtained to construct an immense reservoir at Kokine, north of the city. Once the distribution of clean water was underway, it was noticed that the number of cases of cholera dropped dramatically. Nevertheless, Europeans and the better educated non-Europeans, continued to have their drinking water boiled and filtered. Among the former, the use of soda water became increasingly popular. In the shops and markets of Rangoon, foreign and native-made stone-ware filters were now available.

For the British civil servants and merchants in their spacious houses outside the crowded city, life was pleasant. Almost all these residences were set within spacious compounds which were planted with trees and shrubs. It was said at the time that parts of Rangoon could have been mistaken for a hill station somewhere in India. Each building was of wood, and was supported by sturdy teak posts which had been liberally coated in thick earth-oil to prevent attacks

The Strand Road, Rangoon.

by termites. Even the wooden shingles of the roofs were soaked in this preservative. The ground floor was usually enclosed in lattice work, and was sometimes used for storage purposes.

In the living area on the first floor, the partitions which separated each room did not reach the ceiling, and were only about eight feet in height, allowing air to circulate. Almost all the houses had large enclosed verandahs in which exotic plants were grown. Snakes and other reptiles were often found in this area.

Among the merchants, those dealing in rice became extremely wealthy, the most prominent personality being James Leishman, the 'Paddy King', who made his fortune during the Indian Famine in the 1870s. His extravagant soirees became legendary among members of the entertainment-starved Rangoon society. For many of the British, surrounded by obsequious Indian servants, a lifestyle unavailable to them in England could be lived here to the full.

Good fortune was to smile even more on the mercantile community with the opening of the Irrawaddy Valley State Railway in 1877, resulting in the predictable increase in trade, and the setting up of new businesses. Understandably, as competition increased, some of the older established companies resented the successful new arrivals who were considered too pushy.

Reliable transportation systems also meant that the reputation of Rangoon's markets were growing and farmers from the surrounding districts realized that they could find a more lucrative outlet for their produce. Although a Municipal Bazaar was established at Botataung, at the eastern end of the city, it proved unpopular and lasted only six months.

In 1876, the city authorities decided to set up another market on the waterfront. This was at the western end of the Strand, a former slum area which was now cleared and redeveloped. The choice for the site was a success; being on the river bank meant that perishable commodities could be unloaded from the country boats which tied up alongside. But when the huge building finally opened for business, applications were received from only a few traders, until it was discovered by the Market Committee that the Burmese and Indian managers of rival bazaars were preventing their stall holders from moving to the new site. Needless to say, appropriate and stern measures were taken.

The market complex, which boasted a splendid fountain, consisted of a series of long sheds with corrugated iron roofs, a necessary precaution against fire, but this also meant that the interior was like an oven during the hot season. Nevertheless, the dimly-lit and noisy corridors soon came to be crowded with stalls, customers and hawkers. In each shed a particular commodity, such as rice, cooking utensils, textiles, fish or meat, was sold. There was also a section for food stalls which had on sale meals prepared by the various minorities. A great variety of fresh vegetables could also be had, and it is interesting to learn that in the 1870s, *ah-lu* (potato) which is not indigenous to the country had still to be imported from Calcutta.

Among the poultry and various types of birds for sale, doves and crows could also be found, these were a speciality among the older generation of Burmese, who considered the flesh to be medicinal. Poultry was always sold live and was killed just before a meal was prepared - a necessity in a tropical climate. Like markets everywhere, those in Rangoon burst into life at the crack of dawn, with activity gradually tailing off as the day wore on and the heat increased.

As almost all the Europeans relied on their Madrassi butlers to do the shopping, they were invariably over-charged, and, provided the man was not too greedy, such misdemeanours were overlooked. Often these men would meet at the bazaar and before leaving agree among them-

The first railway in British Burma. Opening of the Rangoon and Irrawaddy State Railway at what was later to become the Phayre Street Station. The crowd on the right is made up mainly of Indians. Europeans and Burmese ladies can be seen on the left. *The Graphic*, June 23 1877.

၁၈၇၇ခုနှစ်တွင်ဖွင့်လိုက်သော ရန်ကုန်မှ ပြည်မြို့သွား မီးရထား

selves the fictitious prices they would present to their *memsahibs*. It was common knowledge at the time that the sole aim in life of these domestics was to make as much money as quickly as possible - before they were discovered and sacked.

Past the Municipal Market and halfway down the Strand Road, was the Chinese quarter. Although the facade of the houses which were built in the traditional style differed in design, they were all of the same height, the reason being that at the time it was not considered proper for one man to raise his head higher than his neighbour; such modesty was to change within a few years. While the main entrances of some of the buildings had folding doors with iron bars, others were open to the elements during the day. At night, the doorways were secured with wooden shutters which were slotted into place and locked. The front room on the ground floor was used as a display area for merchandise, with the living quarters at the back and on the first floor. Almost all the houses contained ancestral shrines in the inner recesses, where joss sticks smouldered, and vases of flowers brightened the gloom.

In the streets of China Town there were tea shops, restaurants, and many confectionery and food stalls. Although Europeans rarely patronized these eating places, there was one establishment, Pinthong and Friends, which drew the younger Englishmen. Here it was possible to obtain or order almost any article of European manufacture. Such competition did not please the vast British-owned departmental stores in central Rangoon. The obliging Chinese proprietor who had various business interests became extremely wealthy. His son, Lim Ching Hsong, the rice merchant, became even wealthier, and built an enormous private residence in the traditional Chinese

OLD RANGOON

Rangoon. The Strand.

Left: Strand Road under construction.

၁၈၇၀ခုနှစ်လောက်တွင်ရှိက်ကူထာ သောအဆို ရရဲ့ ကြီ များ

Above: The Strand Hotel, built 1901, then and in its restored state today

A Burmese Village Street.

style which came to be known as the Ching Hsong Palace. This extraordinary building, with its pagoda-like ninety foot high tower still survives at Kokine, four miles north of the city centre.

For the European residents and visitors, examples of Burmese crafts could be obtained from shops conveniently sited in Edward Street. Here lacquerware, gilded chests, woven textiles, and other objets d'art could be purchased. Many of the artisans lived on the upper floor, and used the large single room at street level as a workshop and showroom. The street was also visited by the Burmese, as some of the vendors catered for the needs of the Buddhist clergy, selling such items as images, religious texts, robes, fans, rosary beads and other paraphernalia. Although the majority of the Buddha images were the handiwork of craftsmen from Upper Burma, some were now being produced locally.

The writer, Gordon, said in his *Our Trip to Burmah* that the Buddha images wore "a very pleasant expression - some being decidedly cheery, others actually jolly, as if determined not go home till morning". He noticed that the Burmese, man, woman, and child, were "happy and pleasant-looking" and were civil and prepared to perform any little service when requested. Gordon was convinced that this characteristic had been replicated in the faces of the Buddha. Considering that images were readily available in Edward Street, one European observer who wandered onto the terrace of the Sule Pagoda commented that although the shrine was teeming with worshippers, unlike other places of worship, there were no Buddha images to be found on the entire platform.

In the area around Edward Street the houses were built tightly packed together. Many were of timber, with only a number of brick structures gracing the street. This meant that when fires broke out it was extremely difficult to bring them under control. The city fathers possibly had a premonition, for in 1875, four manual fire-engines were acquired. These machines were of a primitive design and had to be pulled by volunteers, who, according to newspaper accounts were highly disorganised, whilst an inadequate supply of water for the pipes was transported in barrels on bullock carts. Not surprisingly such machines were quite impotent at bringing under control a series of devastating fires that occurred between 1877 and 1880. The situation was not helped by the attitude of Burmese and Indians who had the curious habit of detachedly standing by and watching their property burn down. Though two new fire-engines were soon imported, they proved to be too heavy for even the strongest pair of horses. The inadequacies of this poorly or-ganised service were to continue to prove a trial for the city for some time to come.

In the 1870s the majority of policemen were drawn from among the Indian community, though a few Burmese, Karen, and Mon officers, inspectors, and head constables, were also start-ing to be appointed. Surprisingly, in 1874, the entire police force in Rangoon numbered only 245 men, and by 1880 had increased to a mere 300. The number dismissed for misconduct con-tinued to rise whilst at the same time robberies and murders also increased. This was partly blamed on the ease with which arms could again be acquired.

Although the citizens of Rangoon were used to reading reports of murders, they was shocked to learn of the brutal killing of the Governor of the Rangoon Jail by some of the convicts. This was to result in the tightening of security and the introduction of a stricter and somewhat brutal regime. Within the high walls, discipline was maintained by flogging, or endlessly treading on the wooden slats of a huge treadmill, while guards who used their canes freely stood behind the men. Contemporary photographs show vicious looking Indian warders, armed with heavy sticks posing over cowed and heavily shackled Burmese convicts.

There were more than two thousand inmates at the jail consisting of Europeans and a medley of Asian races. While the former spent their days breaking stones, the latter were taught a variety of trades, with an emphasis on furniture making, carving, and canework. Their customers were mainly Europeans, who were impressed with the high quality of their work. As the authorities had at their disposal an inexhaustible supply of virtual slave labour, the jail also housed a printing department, and a bindery, where government and commercial publications were prepared.

Elsewhere in the city, the American Baptist Mission also maintained a printing press, and em-ployed a multi cultural workforce to print and bind works in English, Burmese, and in the lan-guage of some of the ethnic minorities. There were also Burmese owned printing houses, such as the *Burmah Herald* (*Myanmar-than-daw-sint*) which had published in 1871, the *Mani-yadana-*

Rangoon Jail — Prisoners carrying out their breakfast.

SEIN KHO. (FAMOUS DANCER.)   No. 80.

Right: "Group of Karen men and women, taken at Rangoon, 1871." Only one young man (holding a large crossbow) is seen wearing his national costume of white home-spun material, the rest of the men have adopted the Burmese style of dress. Although the four women in the centre still wear the traditional smock, their skirts are of Burmese origin.   ၁၈၇၁ခုနှစ်မှကရင်အမျိုး သာ နှင့်အမျိုး သွီ တစ်စု

pon-kyan a collection of historical accounts in three volumes. This was a best seller at the time. The 1870s will long be remembered as the decade when printed books and pamphlets in Burmese became extremely popular, with subjects ranging from historical and religious works, to sciences, novels, and the most sought after of all - plays.

In British Burma, the Burmese theatre was enjoying a strong revival, and as Rangoon was a wealthy port, many of the travelling theatrical companies from the outlying regions converged on the city to take up residence in the Burmese quarter of Kemmindine. By nature a hospitable people, it is a Burmese custom to entertain friends lavishly, and now that most families felt secure with regular employment, theatrical troupes were in demand during the dry and cool seasons. The performance to which all were welcome was usually staged opposite the house of the benefactor, with hundreds of people seated on mats spread on the ground. This meant that the entire street had to be closed to traffic until dawn, when the show ended.

In 1877, *The Graphic* reported that the "assumption by Her Majesty [Queen Victoria] of the title Empress of India has called forth much spontaneous and enthusiastic loyalty throughout the

A BURMESE BAND, CONSISTING OF DRUM,
CYMBALS, CLAPPERS, PICCOLO, TRIANGLE, etc.

"Illustrated Missionary News," 1d. monthly
58, Lewisham Park, S.E.

A Burmese Bath-chair

A family group of Shan-Burmese. The expensive *pasoe* (waist cloth) worn by the two young men (left) and the richly woven *htamein* (skirt) seen on the ladies indicate their middle class background. The photograph is dated 1896.

၁၈၉၆ခုနှစ်မှရှမ်၊မြန်မာမိသာ:စု၊ ထိုခေတ်မှအထူ:ခေတ်စါ:ခဲ့သော လွန်:ရာကျပုဆို:နှင့်ထဘီများ:ကို ၀တ်ထာ:ကြသည်

Indian Empire, each race celebrating the event in its own national and characteristic style. Accordingly on this occasion the inhabitants of British Burmah recognised an opportunity for amusing themselves and at the same time showing their loyalty to Her Majesty. The result was a series of entertainments, combining dramas, dancing, singing, and last, but not least, a religious ode commemorative of the occasion. At such events, or when solemnising some religious festival, it is usual for the younger ladies to act and dance in public; these gatherings included daughters and other relatives of the highest and most influential members of the Burmese community".

In the larger towns, temporary theatres were built and theatrical performances held for the duration of the festivities. King Mindon even sent his court dancers to perform in Rangoon, much to the delight of the Burmese people. Meanwhile, there were also other entertainments in the city, where it was rare to see a female face in the crowd. *The Illustrated London News* said that a prize-fight had been held on the platform of the Shwedagon, between the "Rangoon Pet and the Moulmein Slasher." This contest was well attended by men of all races, as can be seen in the illustration which accompanied the short article; it is interesting to note that an English police sergeant in British Burma wore the same uniform as his contemporaries in London.

Another sport which had become popular since its introduction in 1873 by the author, George Scott, was association football. *The Singapore Free Press* stated that the first football match played in the province was between the boys of St John's College in Rangoon and those of St John's in Moulmein. In 1878, it was Burmans versus the Europeans and surprisingly, considering it was a new game with strange rules, the former won.

In 1879, two of the favourite teams were known wittily as the "*Putsoes* and Trousers"; the former is the name for the sarong worn by a Burmese male. Later, there were the "*Ta-myo-daw-tha-do*" (Sons of a Foreign City: young Europeans) and the "*Kyaung-daw-tha-do*" (Students from the 'Royal' School). Football matches were well attended, and when goals were scored the non-European spectators were liable to vent their feelings with the "wildest shows of emotion".

Gordon said that despite the availability of beer and other intoxicants, drunkenness in a Burmese crowd was rarely to be seen, which was not the case in the seaport towns of England. He noted that beer was already being brewed in Rangoon by the late 1860s, and was declared to have been "very good". The hops, however, had to be imported from England, and sugar from Penang, indicating that the latter was not yet being produced in the country. On the other hand, isinglass, which was used to clarify the brew, and which was obtained from the swimming bladders of fishes, was available locally. Within a few years, the Burmese had acquired a taste for beer and regarded it as a medicine. A certain amount of market-research appears to have been undertaken by the British owners, for the brightly coloured labels were specially designed with the Burmese customer in mind.

Among the British, walks along the winding paths of the Cantonment Gardens, or Dalhousie Park were popular. During the cool season a Regimental Band could sometimes be heard alternately at each of these places during the week. The Royal Lakes was also another favourite spot, as it was close to the cantonment. One visitor in the early 1870s reported seeing long-armed gibbons in the thickly wooded areas near the barracks, but was not sure if they were pets kept by some of the British soldiers. For the European residents of Rangoon, there was also a choice of the two leading clubs - the Pegu and the Gymkhana - where the evening could be rounded off in congenial surroundings.

The Pegu Club, which was founded in 1871, began in a bungalow in Cheape Road. It was originally exclusive and was intended for the senior members of the community; non-Europeans

'Teak Wallahs': employees of the Bombay Burma Trading Corporation. One of the leading timber firms in Rangoon which was founded in the early 1860s. Photographed c.1890s.

မြန်မာကျွန်းနှင့်အသက်မွေးခဲ့ကြသော ဘောင်ဘေဘားမားကုန္ပဏီမှ အင်္ဂလိပ်အရာရှိများ

Cantonment Gardens, Rangoon

Rangoon. Dalhousie Park.

were effectively barred from its premises. But with the growing number of Europeans settling in Rangoon its committee realised that it could no longer be too selective as to the status of a prospective member. In 1882, as membership increased, it moved to larger premises in Prome Road.

Like the Pegu Club, when the small building which housed the Gymkhana first opened its doors in the 1870s, membership was restricted to the military and civil community. The only natives to be seen within the grounds of both these clubs were the docile Indian servants. In the commercial sector of Rangoon there were the Burma Club, where all the heads of firms had their lunch, and the Civil Service Club in Barr Street. Dr Marks, who lived in the city during the late 1860s, commented in his *Forty Years in Burma*, that the successful British merchants and the heads of departments were "our local aristocracy".

At certain times of the year there were Drag hunts in Rangoon. The two famous personalities of the group who used to ride in their "toppers" were a Mr and Mrs Watson, proprietors of a high class barber's shop for Europeans. It is also known that hunts were held once a week "in the rains" [Monsoon]; this must have been uncomfortable as the ground would have been extremely muddy.

For those less strenuously inclined, the extensive and well kept gardens of the Agri-Horticultural Society, that later provided the site for the present General Hospital, was a welcome quiet retreat. Nearby was the country's first museum which had been opened in 1871, and was named after Sir Arthur Phayre, the Chief Commissioner; the building was sited opposite his former residence. It was a magnificent wooden structure - a curious mixture of Victorian and Burmese styles. Like all buildings of the colonial period, the large hall at ground level was covered in trellis panels, while the top floor had a wide verandah surrounding the suite of rooms containing some of the exhibits and a small library.

Contemporary accounts noted that it housed an indifferent collection of objects, which included coins, implements from the Stone Age, instruments, textiles used by the various ethnic groups, and a small section of natural history specimens. Many of the objects had been donated by the European residents. If the quality of the exhibits were not up to standard that was hardly surprising, for the museum had to survive on an annual Government grant of £10! In the late 1880s, some of the earliest and most magnificent Brahmanic sculptures from the Thaton region were displayed here but were of little interest to the general public of the day.

"The Island Pavilion in the Cantonment Gardens." A photograph by Peter Klier who sometimes included his white-clad Indian servant in his pictures. c.1890s.

ကန်တော်မင်ဥယျာဉ်၊ ၁၈၉၀ခု နှစ်လောက်တွင်ရိုက်ကူးထားသည်

A Burmese girl.

[The] ...marked contrast existing between the women of Burmah and those of most of the Indian races include amongst other noticeable features the European-like freedom and absolute equality that the former enjoy, resulting, as might naturally be expected, in an independence of thought and conduct which renders them greatly attractive to foreigners.

THE GRAPHIC, MARCH 24 1877

The opening up of a new province meant that civilian, government, and military personnel, many of whom were unattached males, were arriving in ever increasing numbers. Once installed, quite a few followed the practice adopted during the First Anglo-Burmese War of finding mistresses from among the local women. The trend had begun in India when, before the arrival of the *memsahibs*, Englishmen were accustomed to take an Indian *bibi* (mistress). In those days it was a male orientated society where the men had everything their own way, and relations with the subject Indian races were on a good footing.

Such freedoms, however, were not to last. With the arrival from England of a wife - who had a habit of interfering, or trying to influence her husband concerning either his work, or his attitude towards the Indian - things were never to be quite the same again. Added to this were the over zealous missionaries, who began to appear in India from 1813 onwards. As a consequence, new pressures were brought to bear on the British male against consorting with native women. Some missionaries of the 'fire and brimstone' variety adopted the rather disconcerting habit of visiting the brothel quarters of the cities. There they sang hymns and tried their best to disrupt 'trade', even publishing the names of Englishmen seen in the vicinity.

It was claimed that the local Burmese girls were prepared to take up with men of any nationality, provided the right amount of money was handed to their parents. An Englishman was considered the finest catch, but this had its problems, for many of the girls knew that they and their children would not be acknowledged, and be left behind when their partners returned to England to marry. On the other hand, to be called a *bo-gadaw* - lady of a white man, or a *min-gadaw* - lady of an official had a certain attraction and brought prestige within her circle.

Once installed, the Burmese wife was accorded the deference suitable to her station, from all the non-Europeans with whom she came into contact and whilst she and her Englishman were together her privileged station would be used to her best advantage. In the eyes of her own people she was a legitimate wife and even when the liaison was over she would never be regarded in any way as having been immoral or degraded. Almost all the ex-mistresses of Europeans eventually married Burmese men.

As early as 1872 Government had become alarmed at the increase in the number of children of Burmese mistresses of Englishmen and felt it necessary to send a confidential circular to all civil servants warning them of the consequences. To the irritation of the Chief Commissioner this was not taken seriously. At the Rangoon races, it even led to the appearance of two ponies called 'Chief Commissioner's Confidential Circular' and 'Physiological Necessity'; the latter won the race to the delight and intense amusement of the racegoers.

In the outlying districts many Eurasian children were sometimes abandoned by their English fathers, leaving the mother and her family to bring up the child as best they could. Such children grew up as Buddhists, wore Burmese clothes, and generally led reasonably contented lives. Others, who were sent as boarders to a Christian school by a conscientious father were taught to dress in the Western style and behaved as if they were Europeans.

A few of the leading missionaries were so appalled to learn that some of the abandoned children were being brought up as 'heathens' that plans for an orphanage were soon drawn up. The organisation which led the way was the Diocesan Orphanage for Boys, and it soon took under its wing as many as one hundred youngsters. Their mothers, who were unable to support them, were often only too relieved to hand them over to the care of the missionaries.

At first, the very idea of an orphanage for the "veritable waifs and strays of Burmah" was strongly objected to by government officials, and the leading European citizens of Rangoon. Some claimed that it would "condone immorality and promote concubinage". Fortunately, intense pressure from Dr Marks resulted in funds eventually becoming available, and the orphanage finally won the support of the Government and certain members of the merchant community. The more fortunate among the Burmese women who were financially independent insisted on bringing up their children on their own, providing them with the best education available at the time.

Life for the average Eurasian was usually stressful. As adults, they found it difficult to be accepted socially by the English, who adopted a contemptuous and condescending attitude towards them. The Burmese, on the other hand, were more tolerant - provided they did not adopt too grand an attitude and behave like Europeans. Many married within their own group, and rarely achieved prominence in any chosen field during the latter half of the nineteenth century.

A Burmese Lady of Rank at Home.

Nevertheless, Europeans were to comment on the marked difference in character between the Eurasians who had come over from India, and those of Burma. Civil servants among the former were invariably offensive to the Burmese people in their dealings with them and behaved in a harsh dictatorial manner.

Until the early 1900s, the term Anglo-Burmans meant British men and women who either worked in or were residents of Burma, but soon, it came to mean people of mixed race; the word Eurasian was dropped as it was considered offensive. Over the years, several more circulars against the keeping of Burmese mistresses were issued by the Government. Once again, these were dismissed as an interference in private affairs and led to several Englishmen legally marrying the girls they were living with.

When taking a foreign husband, the second choice for a Burmese girl was a Chinaman. To wed a citizen from the *pyi-gyi* or Great Country was quite acceptable, for it was known that as a husband he not only provided stability, but through industry and business acumen, life in his household would invariably be easy. Burmese wives of the Chinese were usually plump and sleek, and clothed in silks and jewels. In such a union, the boys were brought up as Chinese, complete with a pig-tail, and the girls as Burmese.

Although Hindus and Muslims were acceptable as husbands, they were looked down upon by the Burmese as being inferior. To be called a *kala-mayar* (wife of an Indian) was a denigrating term, even the wealth and social standing of one's husband could not protect a lady from such a title - which the malicious usually uttered with a downward turning of the corners of the mouth. The children of a union between a Muslim-Indian and a Burmese woman were called Zairbaddi by the Indians, but it was also noticed by others that the majority were invariably blessed with good looks and intelligence, and were among the foremost traders in the country.

This curious sense of superiority amongst the Burmese was to be commented on by a bemused *The Times of India*. The paper noted that the feeling was:

> universally entertained by the Burmese for the natives of India. They look on them as a race of slaves, only fit for menial work. They pay no attention to the differences of race and religion existing among them, but class them all together under the name of *kala* (foreigner), a word always uttered in a tone of supreme contempt. [It added that] ...the Indians in turn look down on the Burmese as a totally uncivilised race of jungle-wallahs (people of the jungle), whose ignorant contempt for Indians can only excite laughter, not resentment.

The local press, such as the *Rangoon Daily Mail* and *Daily Review* which were founded during the second half of the 1870s, freely criticised the social scene whilst highlighting the inadequacies of the over burdened Municipal Committee. Other newspapers available in the capital were the *Burma Herald*, *The Times* and *The Gazette*. The citizens of Rangoon also enjoyed a magazine called *Our Monthly* which began publishing from 1880, and another newspaper called the *Rangoon Gazette*.

In 1881 Rangoon was diverted by a well documented case of poltergeist activity, which occurred at the residence of Daw Phaw and her four teenage daughters, in 21st Street. Within the house items of clothing were set on fire and stones thrown. This naturally attracted the curious, who stood for hours on end in front of the building. Those who were admitted, and who had come "from all parts, received pinches so severe as to make a visible bruise; if the visitor said "I under-

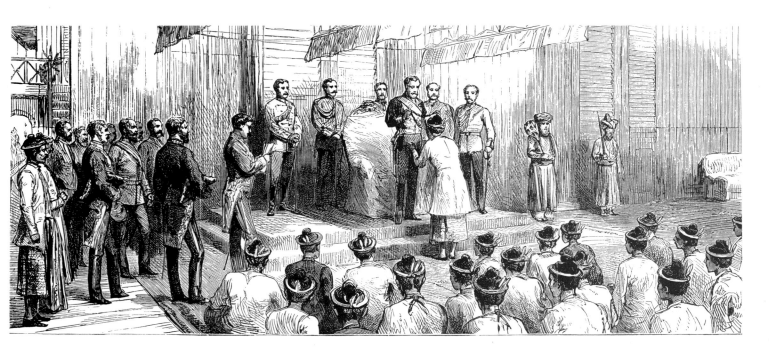

"The Viceroy of India's visit to British Burmah — Lord Ripon decorating Burmese officials at Rangoon." *The Graphic*, March 4, 1882. The ceremony was held in the Durbar Hall of Government House, during which the officials were awarded medals and golden *salwe* (chains of office). Note the punkhas.

stand that only the inmates of the house are pinched," he was certain to get immediately a very hard pinch or smack". The unnerving activities were reported to have continued for eighteen months. Others said that such phenomena, albeit in a milder form, occurred "regularly" but had not been made public. Among the Burmese it was believed that those who suffered such visitations were living on land on which either a pagoda or a monastery had once been built, and that the ancient spirit guardians were making their presence felt.

These spirits must also have taken a dislike to the Municipal Committee, for administration problems began to increase. It would appear that among the committee members the exciting sense of euphoria which once existed was beginning to evaporate. Meetings of the various subcommittees were rarely attended as members found excuses to stay away.

It was not until 1882 that the Chief Commissioner adopted a new system of electing members to the Rangoon Municipal Committee, among whom were leading members of the various communities.

Although enthusiasm was briefly revived, the old apathy gradually returned. This was blamed on the attitude prevalent at the time in which the aim of the transient mercantile community, which included Europeans and Orientals, was to stay in the country to make full use of the financial advantages, and then leave. For those genuinely interested in the improvement of Rangoon, the behaviour of these 'birds of passage' must have been frustrating, and the resolution of the innumerable problems appeared at times to be impossible.

However, many of the problems were brushed under the carpet when Lord Ripon, the Viceroy of India decided to come on a state visit to Rangoon in 1882. In the city, fanciful arches were

Next: pediments and portals — architectural glimpses of 'Downtown' today.

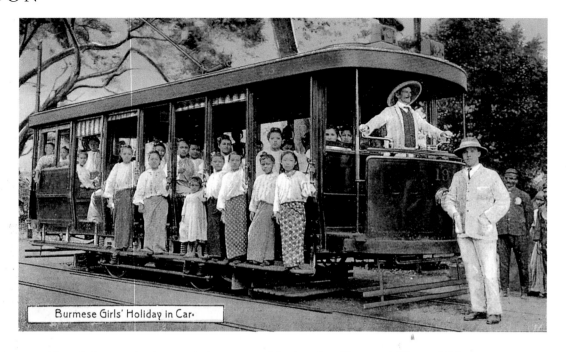

Burmese Girls' Holiday in Car.

erected and thousands thronged the streets. *The London Illustrated New*s of February 18 1882 gave a description of the reception at Government House. The entertainment:

> included the special treat of a grand "Pooay" or *pwe* — a native Burmese theatrical exhibition, combining the features of a dramatic musical and Terpsichorean performance, opera and ballet, all extravaganza, by a select company of amateurs and professionals, who did much credit to their national talent, while giving a lively idea of the peculiarities of national taste."
>
> The dancing, however, was carefully regulated with a view to English notions of propriety; and the graceful damsels who appeared on the stage, posturing with measured motions to the music of a powerful orchestra, were daughters of the most respectable Burmese families, altogether different from the socially inferior class of hired dancing-girls. They were attired in robes of ample drapery, with elaborate coronets or headdresses, and gold chains and other decorations, which did not impede the stately movements — rather of the arms and hands than of the feet, with frequent rising and bowing, alternately, and swaying the head and shoulders to the right or to the left — by which they captivated the eyes of an assembly of spectators. There was nothing violent or unladylike in this performance.

The music, however, was something else, "and though, indeed, delightful to the Burmese ear, was not such as we are accustomed to hear in Europe; the clang of cymbals and tom-toms, the drone of long trumpets, and the beating of drums, made a discordant din which could just be endured, but which none of us could have enjoyed".

After the departure of the viceregal party Rangoon returned to normal, and so did the problems bedevilling the Municipal authorities. During this period, the streets of Rangoon were reported to be either "filthy" or "scrupulously clean". These contradictory statements imply that the quality of the work performed by sweepers fluctuated, and depended entirely on the enthusiasm of those in charge at the time. The situation was also exacerbated in 1882 with the transfer of the police department from the Municipal Committee to that of the provincial government. Where once the constables kept an eye on such mundane matters as litter being thrown in the streets, and other petty offences, they now turned a blind eye, as they felt that it was no longer their duty.

Understandably, complaints were made to the Municipal Committee and the police, although it was known that in the case of the latter, part of the problems were caused by lack of proper supervision, low wages, and insufficient number of personnel. Fortunately, in 1884, under the able administration of Captain Anderson, the Deputy Commissioner, constables' duties became more clearly defined. They were authorized either to arrest or impose fines on offending members of the public, with the result that the appearance of the capital once again changed for the better.

The streets of Rangoon were laid with a metalled central track which was reserved for horse carriages, with the unmetalled strips on both sides being used by bullock carts. During the dry season the heavy wheels of these transport vehicles produced clouds of billowing dust, while in the rains the ground was churned into thick mud. The repair and maintenance of these thoroughfares was to be a constant headache for the Municipal Committee.

Until the early 1880s, the only forms of transport were horses, horse-drawn vehicles, and bullock carts, which were either privately owned or for hire, but in 1884, the first steam-tramway

The caption on the photograph says that this is a 'Burmese Public Carriage'; the box-like structure is based on the Indian *gharry* (horse carriage). In the background can be seen houses built of inflammable materials such as bamboo and thatch, many of the disastrous fires in Rangoon invariably began in such a structure. c.1890s. ရန်ကုန်မြို့ မြန်မာရပ်ကွက်များ တွင်သုံ လေ့ရှိသောဘီဒိုလှည်

was inaugurated by J W Darwood. The important event was reported in the local papers, including the *British Burma News* which was founded in that year.

The tramline began in the Strand from where it turned into China Street and terminated at the southern entrance to the Shwedagon. The tram consisted of an engine with a long funnel, and two carriages attached. Passengers who sat on the open-air deck of the first carriage were liable to be showered with sparks and soot. Behind this was another carriage with a roof, but no side panels to provide protection against the elements; each carriage was attended by a pair of ticket collectors. The novelty of riding on a tram was such that many prospective passengers had to be turned away. For a time, too, the company generously waived fares during the more important Buddhist feast days, which were celebrated on the Shwedagon, but such generosity could not be maintained for long. This form of transportation became so popular that within a few years other lines were extended within the city.

In 1884 a railway line was built linking Rangoon and Toungoo, which was on the frontier of Independent Burma. This was of immense benefit to the mercantile community, as it gave them easy access to a number of large towns and villages which were once difficult to reach.

As the population of Rangoon steadily increased, the major problem of water supply was partly solved with the formal opening of the Kokine Reservoir by the Chief Commissioner. On that day most of Rangoon was in a holiday mood and travelled out to the area in convoys of horse-drawn carriages and carts; a train service was also available for part of the way.

The numerous entertainments included a *yein pwe* (chorus dancing) by a group of young

The Boat Club on the Royal Lakes. This was the original wooden building which had to be extended and rebuilt several times to accommodate the growing number of members. c. 1880s.

၁၈၈၀ခုနှစ်လောက်မှအင်္ဂလိပ် လူမျိုး များ သာသုံ နိုင်ခွင့်ရရှိသော ကန်တော်ကြီ မှလှေအသင် ကလပ်

Burmese Pilgrims

Burmese girls, boxing, wrestling, and boat races. A replica of a magnificent royal barge, with elaborately decorated figureheads of two *karavika* (mythical birds) floated on the reservoir. The vessel carried a tapering multi-roofed pavilion crammed with dignitaries who were rowed across the placid surface to the strains of the traditional 'water music' of the Burmese court. In the early 1880s, riding in a barge of this description in Theebaw's Mandalay would have been a treasonable offence, but here in British Burma nobody gave it a thought, and everyone enjoyed themselves that day.

Despite the grand ceremony, complications with construction work arose, and the water supply could not be laid on for another year, and then only in restricted areas. For a time, the rest of the inhabitants had to make do with wells, or avail themselves of privately-owned water carts which delivered on a daily basis. Perhaps in anticipation of water mains being laid along the thoroughfares, the authorities decided to establish a permanent fire brigade, although it still depended entirely on the goodwill of volunteers; this system was to continue until 1896. Plans for the erection of a fire station were also put into hand, and more up-to-date equipment procured. Predictably, numerous fires continued to occur in the city during the dry season, with huge amounts being lost by all sections of the community.

In the Burmese quarter, where many of the houses were of wood and thatch, there were often scares about pyromaniacs during the dry season. At the height of the panic, a small hut would usually appear at the entrance to a street, and young men formed themselves into groups to keep a night watch on a rota basis; those who were abroad after dark were challenged. Needless to say, crime figures invariably dropped in the locality during such brief moments of communal solidarity.

Away from the Burmese quarter, and in the western sector of the city, there were numerous lodging-houses for the large gangs of coolies who were still flooding in from India. These men and women had been encouraged to come by those who were determined to turn the fertile flat lands into productive paddy fields. In 1872 the number of coolies registered was 16,000, but by 1881 this had leapt to a staggering 66,000.

On arrival, because of their low caste and being almost destitute, many were easily intimidated into performing the most menial duties. Members of this huge workforce remained in Rangoon for a few days, living in overcrowded and appalling conditions before being dispersed over the

"Life and character in British Burma". A street scene in Rangoon. On the left, a pair of British officers show interest in some Burmese ladies. Early 1880s.

ကိုလိုနီ ခေတ်ရန်ကုန်မြို့ သူမြို့သားများ

Private residence in
Tank Road, Ahlone.
c.1900.

118

Traditional boat races on the Inle Lake — here a team of Intha, the fabled leg rowers from the Inle lake in the Southern Shan States, competes. From the Harcourt-Butler collection (British Library). c. 1920s.

လေ့သဘင်ပွဲတော်မှအင်း သားများ

Delta. In some lodging houses as many as twenty-three men were made to share a room. The timid mentality of these people was such that very few dared to protest, and those who did were either assaulted, or evicted as troublemakers. The landlords who owned these establishments were Burmese, Europeans and Indians, they were more than compensated for the initial outlay of constructing these flimsy dwellings.

It would seem that for years, the Municipal authorities were powerless to enforce improvements or to take action, but in 1885 ninety-three landlords were successfully prosecuted, indicating the enormous scale of this scandalous situation. Despite the prosecutions, the problem was to continue well into the next century.

Rangoon now offered a variety of amusements, racing being one form which was enjoyed by all nationalities. When horse racing began, the jockeys were amateurs and the meetings were only held twice a year; bookmakers were then quite unknown. In 1885, the Autumn Meeting in Rangoon was held towards the end of October for four days, with twenty-one races. By the turn of the century, this had increased to monthly meetings. The majority of horses were owned by Chinese and Indians, with many of the latter enduring the three day trip from India to Rangoon on special occasions.

At appropriate venues, other races consisted of contests between racing bullock carts; or a group of elephants taken from the timber yards; or sleek Burmese canoes. For a time boat races had been banned by Government on the grounds that they encouraged gambling. But in 1881, the writer George Scott, and a Captain Wilson, had organised a Regatta on the Royal Lakes, which was estimated to have been attended by ten thousand people. The event which also included Burmese boat racing became hugely popular. Orientals are inveterate gamblers, and on such occasions, although it was known to the authorities that heavy betting continued in a clandestine manner, they either turned a blind eye, or were powerless to stop it.

Whenever the capital was visited by important personages, it was usual to bring down from the Inle Lake, in the Shan States, its famous rowers. These men propelled their long slim canoes standing in pairs, with one leg hooked around a long oar, and balanced themselves by holding onto a central bamboo bar. The teams either raced each other, or towed the dignitaries in a fantastically shaped golden barge around the lake.

Among the British, some of the younger and more sporty types usually spent the early part of the evening at the Boat Club, which was sited at the western end of the Royal Lakes; like the Gymkhana and the Pegu clubs, this was another preserve of the Europeans. It began as a modest little wooden building in the Burmese style, but within a few years, extensions and improvements had to be made. This included a wider verandah overlooking the lake, which was ideal for parties and lantern-lit dances.

During the day and early evening, light sailing vessels and rowing boats could be hired. In the early 1880s, the club was noted for its rather amusing rules: if your boat sank you were fined for illegal bathing; and if you fell off your boat and climbed back in again, you had to pay a fine for "embarking elsewhere than at the prescribed jetty".

Rangoon society, meaning the British, sometimes gathered at the Assembly Rooms to be entertained. The sprawling wooden building which had survived from the 1850s, had to be frequently repaired, and by the early 1880s was sometimes used as a theatre. Here, "troupes from England performed operettas", and plays were presented by the local amateur dramatic society, under the energetic supervision of a Captain Schuyler.

The beautiful Maggie Rayson who was to become one of the great stars of the Gaiety Theatre in London, certainly had unforgettable memories of Rangoon. During her stay, a violent dispute between the cast and the manager of the company ended with her and several actresses being left stranded in this strange city. Schuyler and his friends gallantly came to her rescue by presenting Gilbert and Sullivan's ever popular *Iolanthe* at the Assembly Rooms, with Maggie in the leading role. It was so well received that the generous proceeds from the several performances enabled her, and her fellow artistes, to return to London.

For the Indian community, there were visiting singers, nautch dancers, and theatrical compa-

European Lady Skating.

European Ladies.

Above: Old wooden house of a Chinese merchant in Chinatown today. Note the similarities with the building in the period postcard adjacent.

Pongyi St. Dramatic Troupe, Rangoon.

nies from the subcontinent, who either performed in temporary theatres, or in the houses or compounds of the wealthy merchants. The Burmese and Chinese, too, were entertained by their own strolling players and highly organised theatrical troupes. Such shows usually lasted all night, and made a tremendous din, so that all those within hearing distance were incapable of getting a wink of sleep.

Rangoon had its endearing, if somewhat eccentric characters. One of these, a Burmese matron known as "Mary of Rangoon" was very much in the tradition of the amusing character, Buttercup, from *H.M.S. Pinafore*. Mary had been a familiar sight to the crews of visiting foreign ships since the 1860s. An account which appeared in *The Times of India*, in November 1885, said that she sold "all sorts" to vessels arriving in port, and had made a fortune. Mary, who spoke fluent English, wore Burmese dress, and was described as a "perfect old coquette". On arrival on board a vessel, she would present every officer with a rose. Just before her departure, she would put on a huge straw hat, a yard across, inspect the crew through her field glasses, wave regally, and move on to the next vessel.

In November 1885, the scene on the Rangoon River would have been one of great activity, as the British prepared for war with King Theebaw (r. 1878-85). All Rangoon was buzzing with excitement and speculation as the military authorities assembled a Burma Field Force, consisting of about ten thousand men. Among the superstitious Burmese inhabitants, the knowing ones claimed that the recent earthquakes, fires, strange cloud formations, and the fact that a tiger had actually swum across the busy river to the crowded city, had been clear portents of the impending event.

Trouble between British Burma and the court of the weakling, Theebaw, had been brewing from the moment he ascended the throne in 1878, and was to increase throughout his reign. The brutal massacres within the palace, his inability to rule his kingdom effectively, and his intrigues with the French and the Italians finally sealed the fate of the Konbaung dynasty. Over seven hundred and fifty thousand of his subjects had migrated into Lower Burma seeking the settled conditions which were attainable under the British.

The call for the annexation of Theebaw's kingdom had begun from the end of 1884, when a large number of the leading citizens of Rangoon, among whom were many influential Burmese, attended a noisy meeting in the Ripon Hall to request the Government to take this course of action. But nothing came of this meeting. On the other hand, the British mercantile community, continued to pursue the matter with vigour, knowing that the increase in trade and the opening up of the vast untapped resources of the kingdom would be of immense benefit to them.

In July 1885, the British government had received alarming news that there were indications that Upper Burma could become a French protectorate, a situation which was intolerable. So it came about that the final excuse for war was grasped by the British, when in August the Burmese court arbitrarily imposed an immense fine on the Bombay-Burma Trading Corporation which had been extracting teak in Upper Burma. The London Chamber of Commerce and its Rangoon counterpart immediately renewed their pressure for annexation. Events now began to move swiftly and on October 22, an ultimatum was dispatched to Mandalay. As Theebaw's ministers, who were strongly backed by his ignorant and wilful queen, Suphayarlat, partly rejected it, the order was given on November 11 for the British flotilla to advance into Burmese territory.

The criminal elements in British Burma were quick to take advantage of the unsettled conditions,

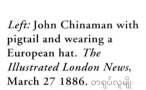

Left: John Chinaman with pigtail and wearing a European hat. *The Illustrated London News,* March 27 1886. တရုပ်လူမျိုး

Right: Burmese Boy. From a sketch by W.H. Titcomb. *The Graphic,* December 19 1885.

and crime in Rangoon and the regions increased during the months leading up to the Third Anglo-Burmese War. While the regular forces proceeded to Mandalay, the city was guarded by the Volunteer Rifles and the police. Surprisingly, among the Burmese in Rangoon, the majority were naive enough to believe that the soldiers of Theebaw were invincible, and would soon retake British Burma. It was reported that two Burmese policemen watching the British regiments in their preparations were heard to comment rather pityingly that these foreigners were in for a shock when they encountered Theebaw's brave warriors, and that they would have no alternative but to run away. Conversely, the feeling among the British was that "we should teach the Burmese, for the third time, that disciplined *kala* troops, both English and sepoy, are not afraid of the rabble Theebaw calls an army".

General Prendergast, who led the expedition, had been clearly instructed by the Foreign Department that once the border at Thayetmyo had been crossed, no submission from Theebaw could be accepted, and that Mandalay was to be occupied and the king deposed.

The British flotilla which steamed up from Thayetmyo in single file was said to have been four to five miles long, and bristling with modern arms. Predictably, the city of Mandalay was taken fifteen days later, and the ex-king and his family were brought down on the steamer *Thooreah* under a strong guard of the Liverpool Regiment. They arrived at Rangoon on December 5, and

Opposite above: A theatrical performance for Burmese envoys, Rangoon. An accompanying photograph is titled "Embassy from Upper Burma". Judging by the quality of the print the photograph is datable to the closing years of King Mindon's reign (1853-78). The reception hall of wood and bamboo was built according to the traditional design allocated to an envoy. Behind this structure were a series of rooms for the ambassador and his suite. The kneeling dancers are all male.

အင်္ဂလိပ်ပိုင် အောက်မြန်မာပြည်သို့ ရတနာပုံရွှေမြို့တော်ကြီး မှရောက်ရှိလာသော သံအဖွဲ့အား အမျိုးသားယိမ်နှင့်ဖျော်ပြေနေပုံ

Opposite below: "Embassy from Upper Burma". The Ambassador and his suite, with two guards wearing brass helmets, and armed with spears. In the background is a *kalaga* (wall hanging of appliqué and sequins) decorated with displaying peacocks, the royal emblem of the later Konbaung kings. Late 1870s.

ရတနာပုံရွှေမြို့တော်ကြီး မှ ရန်ကုန်သို့ရောက်ရှိလာသော သံအဖွဲ့

the "next morning, the *Thooreah* steamed alongside the *Clive*, and a gangway covered in with canvas was placed between the two vessels". The transfer of the royal prisoners was then safely accomplished.

The vessel remained moored in mid-stream for nearly a week. Earlier, some princesses whom Suphayarlat had ill-treated, and who had been brought down from Mandalay in error by the British, were discovered hiding in the water closets of the *Thooreah*. These terrified ladies begged "most piteously" not to be sent to India with the former king and his allegedly cruel queen. To their immense relief, they were released into the care of some of the leaders of the Burmese community.

Contemporary newspaper reports said that crowds flocked to view the steamer. They came either in "sampans filled with respectably dressed Burmese and Indian natives, or gigs with Europeans, and numerous well-packed steam launches surrounded the vessel, but were compelled by the guard boats to keep a respectful distance. The banks of the river were also thronged with natives anxious to obtain a glimpse of the proceedings. All, however, were doomed to disappointment".

Another writer observed that the "owners of steam launches in the river did a brisk business taking people, for a consideration, round the steamer in which Theebaw and his queens were confined" — at four annas a ride.

The Burmese at first refused to believe that the ex-King was really there, but when they realized that it was indeed Theebaw, there was a great wave of sympathy for him and his queens. One newspaper article commented rather acidly that if these "new admirers" of Theebaw felt so strongly about him, why had they not moved up to Mandalay when he reigned there, instead of living, and prospering in the safety of British Burma.

Many Burmese were convinced that the prisoner on board the *Thooreah* was not Theebaw, and that he had been spirited away by his ministers to emerge at some later date to reclaim his kingdom. The proof of their reasoning, they insisted, was that nobody had actually seen him in Rangoon. It was also thought that the story was an attempt at propaganda by the British authori-

The expedition against King Theebaw of Burma - the first of the Irrawaddy Fighting Flotilla. *The Graphic*, December 5 1885.

တတိယ အင်္ဂလိပ် မြန်မာစစ်ပွဲအစ

ties. All these speculations, however, did not stop the curious crowds from lining the river front opposite the vessel.

The British officers who had heard all the lurid tales about the Mandalay court, and were expecting to see an evil looking monster, were surprised when they came face to face with the inoffensive Theebaw. Thirkell White saw the royal couple on board and remarked that "Theebaw was in appearance a Burman of very ordinary type. He looked neither dissipated nor cruel; nor did he show any emotion or feeling for his melancholy position". Whilst he observed that although Suphayarlat "bore no appearance of special depravity, she certainly looked a little shrew". Nevertheless, he was of the opinion that the many stories of her cruelty and wickedness had been much exaggerated.

On January 13 1886, *The Times of India* reported that it was "generally believed that King Theebaw was a drunken debauchee, who committed the most ghastly excesses when under the influence of the juice of the grape or its substitute. This impression appears to be erroneous. A contemporary's Calcutta correspondent met an officer the other day who had recently returned from Burmah in company with Theebaw. This officer assured him that the dethroned monarch

Transfer of the captive King Theebaw from the steamer *Thooreah* to the troopship *Clive* at Rangoon on December 6, 1885. Huge crowds watched from the bank, while some took to the water in numerous small boats. *The Graphic*, January 16 1886.

အား:ခြင်:မမျှရှာသည့်
သီ ပေါဘုရင်လေး:အား:
ကုလား:တိုင်:သို့ပို့ရ့
အင်္ဂလိပ်များပြင်နေကြပုံ

Transport difficulties during the Third Anglo-Burmese War. *The Graphic*, January 16, 1886.

NEW NEIGHBOURS.

Right: "The Burmese Toad". A cartoon, typical of crude imperialist propaganda, which appeared in *Punch* on October 31, 1885. This was just before the fall of Mandalay on November 29. In the background is another toad representing France.

၁၈၈၅ခုနှစ်မှ ကြွားကြွား ဝါဝါ ရေးဆွဲထားသောအင်္ဂလိပ်ကာ တွန်းဆရာတစ်ဦး၏ လက်ရာ

Left: "New Neighbours". A cartoon depicting the annexation of Upper Burma in January 1886. John Chinaman is shown greeting a British soldier with "Me glad to see you here, John, Chin-chin". *Punch*, January 16 1886.

အင်္ဂလိပ်အားကြိုဆိုနေသော တရုတ်စေ့လျော

Opposite: the Customs House on Strand Road.

never touches liquor, and that they tried to tempt him on board with every conceivable sort, from champagne down to gin, without success".

Although some modern Burmese writers have claimed that the royal couple had been forced to leave all their valuables behind in Mandalay, an article in *The Graphic* (Dec. 19 1885) said that Theebaw had "taken away with him jewellery to the amount of four lakhs of rupees, and the Dowager Queen to the amount of half that sum". It is not known what else was hidden on their persons. The report added that "on the following Thursday, the prisoners were transferred to the Government steamer *Canning,* which steamed away for Madras the same night".

After the annexation in 1885, pretenders to the Burmese throne appeared. While some were genuine patriots, the majority were criminals, charlatans, and opportunists. Among them were a Government vaccinator, a Zairbaddi named Yarkut, who called himself the Shwegyobyu Mintha (Prince White Dove); a gull-catcher who styled himself the Setkya Mintha (Prince of the Thunderbolt); and several bogus priests. These men were to prey on towns and villages, torturing and murdering law abiding Burmese citizens whom they claimed were co-operating with the British.

If a marauding band of dacoits obtained news that a village had supplied information against them, the little community was punished with the most ferocious cruelty. Messages left by these retreating murderers for the pursuing British police, were sometimes placed in the mouth of a de-capitated head, with the corpse pinned into a seated position, and holding the head in its lap.

Some of these pretenders styled themselves kings, and lived in thatch huts which they called 'the golden palace'. The appropriate number of 'queens' were installed, and 'ministers' appointed. Under the influence of drugs, some boasted that they could summon vast supernatural armies at will, and distributed bulletproof pills to the rabble which followed them. While the taking of Mandalay in 1885 was described as a 'picnic' by the British, the pacification of the upper part of the country was considerably more arduous, and was not completed until well into the 1890s. Even then, there were occasional outbreaks, which were stamped out with difficulty. The problem was to persist.

A Gem in the Imperial Crown

CAPITAL OF ALL BURMA

FROM 1886

As far as the British mercantile community was concerned, the results of the annexation were phenomenal. Within a few years the number of business establishments increased in the city and the huge profits which were being made were effectively syphoned off. For the Burmese, their status in their own country was now that of second class citizens.

The excitement caused by the annexation had barely died in Rangoon, when the Viceroy, the Marquis of Dufferin, accompanied by his Marchioness, Harriot, decided to visit Burma in February 1886. As their ship drew alongside, a salute of thirty-one guns was fired by the Rangoon Volunteer Artillery, while at the same time theyards were manned on the men-of-war in the harbour. The city was in a festive mood and twenty exotic triumphal arches, double the number erected during the previous Viceroy's visit, were constructed by the various nationalities along the route to the Residence of the Chief Commissioner.

A newspaper report said that the Burmese put up five arches, the Chinese two, Karens one, Moguls two, one each from among the Jews, Chetties, Marwarrees, Suratis, Chulliahs, Moodliars, and four from the British community. So keen was the wish to impress the Dufferins that one of the Indian merchants embellished his entire arch with gleaming small coins and silver rupees.

The viceregal pair remained in Rangoon for a few days and then proceeded up country to enjoy the curious sights of Mandalay. On their return, the usual round of entertainments and the obligatory visits to various institutes followed. The highlight of the tour was the

Burmese Courtship.

Left: Cupola and finials of the Karen Monastery, set in the monastery estates to the south-east of the Shwedagon.

splendid public ball held at the Residence at a cost of 8,000 rupees; at the time, the average coolie working from dawn to dusk only earned nine rupees per month.

Harriot, who has left a fascinating account of their visit in her, *Our Viceregal Life in India*, said that the Rangoon Ball, at which 700 guests were present, was a great success, and that it was held in a huge room with forty doors; supper was served in an enormous red and white marquee in the grounds. At the ball, prominent members from the numerous nationalities of Rangoon - including the Burmese, mingled freely with the British.

Alongside the residence was a long covered walk, a temporary structure which had become extremely popular at important soirees in British India, and known as the *kala jugga* (dark place); the word referred to the numerous dimly lit little arbours on each side, which were well concealed with potted plants and curtains. Harriot concluded that their "scientific arrangements for flirtation" was "unsurpassed". As she made a state promenade down the walk she gave a "shock" to each startled couple within, and even discovered an extremely embarrassed Military Secretary in the last booth.

Harriot went on to describe the Residence as a large sprawling wooden structure with a shingle roof, and a brick annex. The great hall had in its time been a witness to many an unusual incident. To mention but one, during an earlier official reception held for General Ulysses Grant, ex-President of the United States, a senior officer withdrew the chair from behind the Commissioner of Pegu as he was about to sit, this was said to have "brought down the house" - as the unfortunate man weighed about twenty stone.

Many of the bedrooms in the building had lattice panels above the partitions to ensure that cool air circulated. The windows, however, did not have glass panes, which made the room rather dark, but such gloom was believed to have been welcomed in a tropical country where the harsh glare from the sun can be trying. Each room was fitted with a *punkah* (a long strip of cloth on a pole) which was pulled by a *punkah-wallah*. Some of the bedrooms had several of these contraptions, including a smaller one inside the huge mosquito-nets which hung over each bed. Harriot was horrified to find that her room was "swarming with lizards", and that a member of her suite nearly got stung by a scorpion. The spacious dining room was said to have been "quite open", but despite the *punkahs*, everyone complained of the heat.

For the remainder of their visit, sports were held at the Royal Lakes, with boat races being one of the main events. The viceregal party were also entertained with classical dances by the daughters of the Burmese elite who, according to Harriot, performed "very gracefully and nicely".

It is interesting to learn that in 1886 there was already a School of Art in Rangoon, where silver bowls were made and wood carving was taught; curiously, drawing and painting are not mentioned. The Viceroy and his lady visited this establishment, and later, decided to go on a walkabout in the local bazaar to the utter amazement of the crowds and anxiety of the police. Harriot later wrote home to say that her husband had "made a sort of tasting progress through the food bazaar. He tasted pickled tea, and palm-sugar, and betel-nut, and every queer sort of seed or mess he came near, while the Burmese ladies sat aloft amidst their goods and smiled upon him". She was no doubt horrified at the thought that he was laying himself open to all manner of diseases. Fortunately, nothing untoward happened to the Viceroy, and he and his consort returned to India.

Another event during the early part of 1886 was the appearance of the "Mandalay Hairy Family" in Rangoon. They had once been the favourites of the Burmese royal family, but now, deprived of a source of sustenance, a Mr Archer had arranged to have them exhibited in Calcutta, Bombay, and London. The extraordinary pair, Daw Phoon and Maung Po Sin, mother and son, were both covered in thick silky hair, and drew large crowds during their short stay in Rangoon; at the time they were aged sixty-three and twenty-nine respectively. *The Times of India*, said that they were "the fourth generation of the family known to history, and the exhibition relates that each generation has been seven in number, three of each being hairy and the other four displaying no extraordinary phenomena".

The annexation of Upper Burma and the visit of the Dufferins appears to have galvanized the authorities in Rangoon, for as far as amenities were concerned, the improvements were rapid. Within the city, the value of land had increased to such an extent that a small house in prestigious Merchant Street, which was sold in 1885 for 6,000 rupees, was able to command over 55,000 rupees the following year. Though the city was already furnished with a General Hospital, which was claimed to be the best equipped in the East, an additional hospital called the Dufferin was opened in 1887; the former was sited opposite the Anglican Cathedral, while the latter was situated next to the Rangoon Jail.

Travel facilities into the interior also improved, as the railway line from Toungoo was extended to Mandalay in 1888, and completed the following year. This was also of great importance to the military authorities, as it enabled them to move large numbers of troops from Rangoon to the newly acquired but troubled areas in Upper Burma. By the late 1890s other branch lines were opened all over the country.

The inhabitants of Rangoon now enjoyed a plentiful supply of clean water, and most importantly, a modern sewage system was being installed for the entire central area of the city. Tramlines were also being laid along all the principal thoroughfares. One of the most important social events in the city were the increasingly popular race meetings. In March 1886, *The Graphic* reported that;

> the promenade lawn was thronged with the European ladies and gentlemen of Rangoon. The natives, a lively race, fond of any kind of holiday diversion, collected in large numbers, and some of them climbing the trees, hung like birds on the branches, enjoying a capital view. Chinamen, with money in their pockets, one of them dressed like an English country gentleman, cunningly betted on the races, and contrived to win money, as they do in every transaction. The seamen of the Naval Brigade, ever willing to share in any fun that is to be made on shore, rode for a special prize, subscribed for by the officers, contributing much to the general amusement.

With the extensive newspaper coverage of the annexation, the "Land of the Golden Pagodas" was now definitely on the map. Numerous books on the country were in print, in particular George Scott's *The Burman: His Life and Notions*, written under the pseudonym Shway Yoe, had helped to familiarise the British public with the charming Burmese; the book had received impressive reviews in England since its publication in 1882.

The Eighties ended with a visit by H.R.H. Prince Albert Victor, the eldest son of the Prince of Wales. In Rangoon, the route from the jetty to the Residence was again decorated with numerous arches. Regimental bands played, and delicate dancing girls performed in the streets. Within government circles it was whispered that the Prince had been deliberately sent on a tour of British

Wooden residential buildings in the Rangoon suburbs: *above left* is a detail of a house from York (Yaw-mingyi) Road; *below left* a pavilion in the grounds of the Kyun-daw Kyaung; *above* is one of the few surviving teak houses on Boundary (Dhamazedi) Road.

"New Year's Day in Burmah - a sketch at the Water Festival". The festival which lasts for several days involves throwing water which is believe to wash away the sins of the past year. *The Graphic*, January 3 1886.

၁၈၈၆ခုနှစ်မှ သင်္ကြန်ပွဲ

India to avoid being implicated in a scandal involving prominent male members of society and telegraph boys which was about to break in London. The Prince was later suspected of being Jack the Ripper. Fortunately, the 'Children of the Empire' were blissfully unaware of these dark rumours, and were delighted with the Prince. One of Albert Victor's last duties was formally to open the sewage works in Rangoon.

State visits to Burma were to increase, much to the delight of the Burmese craftsmen who specialized in an ancient ephemeral art form known as *sat-panchee*, which involved constructing an assortment of large figures, and fantastic structures, all made out of bamboo, coloured paper and tinsel. Although work was available throughout the dry season from the organisers of the numerous secular and religious ceremonies, commissions from Government invariably meant more money.

The Nineties were ushered in by another outbreak of poltergeist activity. This time the victim was a European who lived in a rented house in Sule Pagoda Road. Although the manifestations were particularly violent, the recipient of all these disturbing activities was reported to have been fascinated. However, he finally had to leave when sand began appearing in his food. The empty house then "attracted great crowds of people including many soldiers".

In 1892, the old wooden Residence which had been considered inadequate as early as 1872 was demolished to make way for a new brick Government House. The building cost £40,000 to build, and was of red and yellow brick and terracotta. The author, G E Mitton, who was a guest, said in her *A Bachelor Girl in Burma*, that it had been "designed to give space and air. The hall runs right up to a dome, and the upper stories are carried round it in a series of white arcades. The handsomely carved teak staircase is in two branches, passing up two sides. The floor is of mosaic, and a high arch opposite the entrance shows a glimpse of one of the most magnificent ball-rooms in the world". She stated that the walls were decorated with "fine specimens of Burmese wood-carving" and other objects; this contradicts present day suggestions that the arts of the country were never given pride of place by the British government.

Mitton noted that while the ground floor was guarded by white-clad Indians, with daggers in their belts, the downstairs servants were mostly Burmans, with "turbans and *lyungyis* of the purest purple, with snowy white *engies* or jackets".

In the city, the reclamation of land in the more important areas had been completed by 1890, with much needed residential quarters, new roads, and tram lines being added to the now sprawling city. However, complaints soon began to increase against the tram company accusing them of high fares, failure to maintain the tracks, and of being a danger to the public.

Added to all this was the hazard from sparks which still belched from the funnel of the engine, and which continued to damage the clothes of passengers. There had also been collisions with horse carriages and pedestrians. Although, in the latter case, it must be said that it was not entirely the fault of the tram driver, for those who suffered injuries were mainly coolies carrying heavy loads on their heads, or nervous country folk on their first visit to a big city. Further complaints and fines by the Municipal Committee finally lead to the introduction of an electric tram-car system in 1906. Europeans, especially the ladies, were not inclined to favour the tram as it would have put them on the same level as the natives.

Another form of public transport which was introduced in 1893 was the rickshaw. At first, perhaps because of the novelty a few memsahibs were seen in the city riding in their private vehicle pulled by an Indian dressed in a curiously designed Indo-Chinese livery. For the ordinary citizen, the commercially run rickshaws were cheaper than the pony-gharries, which before long were monopolized by the city's prostitutes. When this became common knowledge, understandably, neither the memsahibs nor decent women among the non-Europeans could be seen travelling in one. The rickshaws were originally pulled by Chinamen, but gradually they were replaced by Cooringhi or Tamils from India; this form of transport survived well into the 1950s.

For the man in search of nocturnal pleasures, there were a few bars in the city, opium dens in China Town, and secluded little side streets in which the prostitutes from a variety of races plied their trade. These painted ladies sat in the doorways, staring or beckoning to passing males who showed interest. Among the Burmese, the traditional sign which indicated that a woman was a prostitute was the way in which she hung her hair loosely at the back; this was done when she was on display. The notorious Burmese brothel quarter of Dalla, across the river from Rangoon, probably did not survive into the 1890s because of its difficult location and competition from new well-run foreign establishments in the city.

As land prices soared speculators moved in and, to make the maximum use of every available inch of ground, many began buying up older properties which stood within their own compounds. The houses were then demolished and replaced by masonry tenements. Almost all the available space on the water front which encompassed the city on three sides, was given over to the industrialists. The only open area being the strip of land in front of the Strand, backed by an imposing row of public buildings. On the south and western sides of Rangoon, wharves, jetties, warehouses for imported goods, oil depots and refineries, and mills of all types again monopolised the river bank. One of the impressive sights in the timber yards were the trained elephants working with their mahouts among the huge teak rafts which were moored in front of the two

A triumphal arch of bamboo, cloth and paper, erected for the Rangoon Volunteer Artillery as they welcomed Prince Albert Victor, in December 1889.

၁၈၈၉ခုနှစ်တွင် ရန်ကုန်မြို့သို့ ရောက်ရှိလာသော အင်္ဂလိပ်ဝေလမင်း သာ အာ ကြိုဆိုနေကြသော အင်္ဂလိပ်စစ်သာ များ

Above: A Chinese arch constructed by the Hokkien community to welcome the Prince Albert Victor in December 1889.

၁၈၈၉ခုနှစ်တွင် ရန်ကုန်မြို့သို့ ရောက်ရှိလာသောဝေလာမင် သာ အာ ကြိုဆိုရံဆောက်လုပ်ထာ သော တရုပ်မဏ္ဍပ်

Below: A triumphal arch put up by the Chettiyar (Indian moneylender) community to welcome the Prince in December 1889.

၁၈၈၉ခုနှစ်တွင် ချစ်တီကုလာ များ ဝေလာမင် သာ အာ ကြိုဆိုရံဆောက်လုပ်ထာ သောမဏ္ဍပ်

Shipping Elephant.

leading timber companies - the Bombay Burma Trading Corporation and Steel Brothers. Each animal cost between 6 & 7,000 rupees, and spent its day dismantling the rafts and stacking the logs ready for the saw mills.

These thriving companies were owned by Chinese, Europeans, and Indians, the three prominent groups who were responsible for the prosperity of the city. As the mild-mannered and easy-going Burmese had been effectively elbowed out of the way, at the time, ownership of such places in Rangoon was indeed rare for the indigenous inhabitants.

One of the more prominent testimonies which indicated that Burma was fast becoming the 'Rice-bowl of Asia' was the increase in the number of rice-mills on both sides of the Rangoon River. Indeed, in some publications of the period, Rangoon was referred to as the 'Rice City'. These depressing signs of this lucrative industry, with their corrugated iron roofs and tall smoking chimneys were in squalid contrast to the impressive buildings along the Strand, and the great golden pagoda floating above the haze.

Between January and April, huge country craft laden with new paddy converged on these mills. At peak periods the workforce was employed on a shift system for six days and nights, the machinery being switched off only on a Sunday. The mounds of husk produced were conveniently dumped into the river, where great patches either lay rotting in the water or were carried out to sea in long swirling swaths of gold.

The construction of a network of rail links by the prosperous owners also meant that paddy could now be transported from land-locked areas and be processed speedily to be dispatched to the foreign vessels waiting in the Rangoon River. This second form of transportation was to contribute considerably to the rapid expansion of other trades.

Each mill was sited within its own compound, which sometimes contained barrack-like wooden accommodation for its permanent workers. Many of the less-fortunate casual Indian labourers tended to build shacks just beyond the boundary fences, giving rise to intensely crowded and unsanitary conditions. Every now and again these desperately poor little communities would be visited by municipal gangs, who were supervised by the police; amidst screams and cries from the defenceless owners, their homes would be torn down. But within a few months the huts would reappear, and remain untouched until the next blitz.

During the reigns of Mindon and Theebaw, a large number of Burmese peasant families migrated to British Burma to work in the rice fields, but after the annexation, and once peace had been restored, some of these people returned to their villages. As a huge labour force was now needed for the vast rice fields in the Delta, thousands of Indian coolies stepped in to fill the vacuum left by the Burmese.

Many were often confused and apprehensive after a gruelling and uncomfortable journey by sea. Desperate for work, they were overawed by, and completely under the control of the officials from the various organisations which were responsible for recruitment. The practice, during this period, was to sell the services of these workers by auction. Although sympathetic noises were made by those in authority about the existence of what was virtually a slave trade, nothing was ever done to alleviate such exploitation. Among the lower classes of India, word spread that there were great opportunities to be had in the new province of Burma, with the result that by 1891, the Indian inhabitants in the city outnumbered other nationalities, including the Burmese. The exploitation of these foreign workers was to continue.

The heart of the Indian business community began in the western sector of the Strand Road, and was centred in and around Mogul Street. A prominent feature along this busy thoroughfare was the Mogul Musjid, with its white-washed minarets. Facing this massive building of Islam, and as if in defiance, was a gaily painted wooden structure belonging to the Chettiyar, a money-lending class of Hindus. The facade was lovingly carved in the medieval style of South India, and it contained a large hall in which religious and other ceremonies were held.

Another white mosque built on a smaller scale, but architecturally more refined, shared the

Pazundaung Creek.

northern end of the street with an imposing wooden church used by Indian Christians. All available space between these religious buildings were packed with tenements, shops, and offices. Very few Burmese were to be seen in this area. As the Indian quarter consisted of Hindus and Muslims living in close proximity, it was inevitable that there would be encounters over religious issues and in June 1893, during the festival of Bakr-i-id, Rangoon witnessed its first riot - the result of a violent clash between these two communities.

The Muslims provoked a confrontation by insisting on sacrificing a cow, which is held sacred by Hindus, in front of one of their premier temples in 29th Street, a disreputable and overcrowded tenement area of Rangoon. Although the authorities took precautions by having the street guarded by Sowars (mounted military police), in the confusion caused by the swirling mass of fanatical men, the animal had its throat cut. Pandemonium ensued, and fighting broke out everywhere.

In Mogul Street the marble steps of the main mosque and the pavements outside were covered in blood as Hindu and Muslims spurred on by religious intolerance and hate attacked each other. Thirty people were killed during the worst of the riot, in which householders joined in by indiscriminately throwing missiles from their windows; several British officers were hit. A high percentage among the wounded, which amounted to over 200, were the Sowars who were mainly Muslims. The police had no option but to fire on the rioters. Order was finally restored with the greatest of difficulty, and the city settled down to an uneasy peace. For years after, the Indian sector of the city annually bristled with police during the celebration of Bakr-i-id.

This incident was to test to the limit the competence of the police force, which was now divided into a Civil and a Military division, the latter having been created in 1886 to deal with the unrest caused by the annexation of Theebaw's kingdom.

Within the Chinese quarter, which shared a border with the Indian community, the 'Sons of the Flowery Kingdom' kept to themselves, and unlike some of their volatile neighbours were rarely in the news. Among the Europeans, China Town, with its opium dens, eating and entertainment houses, was seen as being exotic and mysterious, and drew the more reckless after dark. The educated and better class of Chinese males had their own clubs, the three most prominent being the Chinese Club in Latter Street, and another of the same name in Canal Street, while the third, the Hong Kong Club, was situated in China Street.

During this period, the sale of opium was a Government monopoly in Burma and India, and by providing shops for habitual opium smokers, who had to obtain a licence, it was naively believed that the formalities would discourage a new generation of addicts. The system, unfortunately, was open to abuse. Many of the addicts resold the good quality opium obtained from the Government shops to illegal dens. Supplies were also smuggled in from China either through the Shan States, or by sea into Rangoon. Although the penalties were severe, the profits were enormous. The Chinese dealers were also past masters in the art of identifying the weaker characters among the police, and corrupting them with suitable bribes.

The encouragement of this terrible vice had begun with the annexation of Lower Burma. Mrs Ernest Hart was to note rather despairingly in her *Picturesque Burma*, that "almost immediately after the annexation, the Indian Government established licenced shops for the retailing of opium, with no restriction as to the number of shops. Rangoon became flooded with men of

仰光中華學堂學生撮影

Chinese School Boys — Rangoon.

Rangoon Rice Merchants.

Downtown: back streets.

every race, and with adventurers of often the lowest character, to many of whom strong drink is the elixir of their excited and dissipated lives. The Indian Government, without due regard of their high duty to the non-abstaining races committed by conquest to their charge, allowed drinking shops, distilleries, and opium dens to be opened in the provinces of Arakan, Tenasserim, and Pegu, in the midst of the temperate but easily tempted Burmans, and seemed to think that the gathering in of a large revenue from liquor and opium justified the disregard of the vices of which it depended."

The effect of this policy was seen in the rapid degeneration of the young Burmans of the annexed provinces; so that in 1862, Sir Arthur Phayre reported that "the effect of the Government measures can only be deemed deplorable and disastrous, and that drinking spirits and smoking opium had become almost universal among the Arakanese [and Burmese] young men."
An official report said that:

the use of this deleterious drug, strictly prohibited in Burmese times, has been considerably on the increase of late. Organised efforts were made by Bengal agents to introduce the use of the drug, and to create a taste for it among the rising generation. The general plan was to open a shop with a few cakes of opium, and invite the young men and distribute it gratuitously. Then, when the taste was established, the opium was sold at a low rate. Finally, as it spread through the whole neighbourhood, the price was raised, and large profits ensued.

Mrs Hart noted that the "best and most respectable of the natives earnestly deplored the growth of the evil, and again and again made representations to the Government on the subject, but in spite of the prayers of all classes, monks and laity the Government of India refused to take any action".

In 1880, the people of Arakan again petitioned the Government to abolish the opium trade, and even offered to pay extra tax for the loss of the opium revenue - but without success. Despite a report *The Times of India* in 1886 on this scandalous situation with the headline "How we poison the Burmese", the Government continued to ignore the criticisms. Mrs Hart said that:

> ... the evil grew at such a pace that, in the five years ending 1890, the excise revenue of liquor and opium increased 80 per cent. The habit of eating and smoking opium grew with surprising rapidity, so that in 1891, the consumption of opium per head of the population was higher in Lower Burma than in any other province of India.

Nevertheless, it should be pointed out that the opium problem was nothing new, Cesare Fedrici said that it was one of the principal imports into Burma in 1567. Even during the strict reign of Badon Min (r.1782-1819), the young men at court were "passionately addicted to liquor and intoxicating drugs, employing secret agents to obtain them at any price, though the penalty was death". Several of the thirty-seven *nat* (spirits) who are worshipped by the Burmese are known to have died of a drugs related overdose. Although all the Commissioners and Chief Commissioners who were in Burma were opposed to the opening of liquor and opium shops, they were powerless to act against the Government in India.

The Nineties brought circuses from England, Europe, and India. Many of the Burmese, although impressed by the gymnastic and other performances, were said to have been shocked at seeing

Downtown back streets.

European ladies in tights and short skirts. There were also regular race meetings, league football, and cricket: the last was beyond the comprehension of the Burmese crowds, who preferred football.

It was inevitable that as the decade progressed the population increased, and the need for housing in Rangoon became acute. The only option for the municipal authorities was to expand in a northerly direction. But a formidable barrier, composed of Government House, military lands, public institutions, and parks effectively sealed in the city. Beyond this band were vast areas from which the jungle and scrub land had still to be cleared. Unfortunately, the three roads which led out of Rangoon were outside the zone in which public transport of any kind operated. As these facilities were confined to the central area, the average citizen, whether office worker, petty trader, or labourer, had no alternative but to continue living as close as possible to his place of work.

For those fortunate enough not to have to depend on public transport this situation did not pose a problem. The British and wealthier non-Europeans were the first to move out towards Kokine, which was still countrified and blessed with the large Victoria Lake (now called Inya Lake). At first such bungalows were used simply as weekend retreats, but soon there was a rush to erect more substantial residential buildings.

The architecture of the European house in Rangoon was never static and appears to have changed with each decade. Some of the newer dwellings were described as being built like Swiss chalets, with eaves scalloped into fretwork designs, and painted white. The drawing room was on the first floor, usually above the porch, and was filled with an assortment of furniture, Burmese and Indian knick-knacks, reminders of Home, and the inevitable *punkahs*.

In such a household, the servants, who were predominantly Indians, consisted of the cook, bearer, *ayah*, maid, house-boy, gardener, sweeper, water-carrier, coachman, *syce*, and night watchman. At the time, though Burmese servants could be found in the homes of wealthy Burmese families, most thought that domestic service with a foreigner was beneath their dignity.

Then as now, outward appearances were of the utmost importance, and it was the preoccupation of garden-conscious Englishmen to present a lush lawn and a well-stocked garden. But the odds were usually against them, as the Burmese sun had a habit of scorching and shrivelling the tender grasses and other plants introduced from cooler climes. The role of the *mali* or gardener, aided by numerous assistants, was to prevent such a catastrophe.

To the rear of the residence was the kitchen which was ruled by the cook. This was a small

District Courts, Strand Road, Rangoon.

Minto Mansions Hotel, Rangoon.

shed which was either built of bricks or with sheets of corrugated iron - a fire precaution - and was connected to the dining room by a long covered passageway. The food was served by a bearer, who was also responsible for setting the table and looking after the crockery.

Almost all the bedrooms had a bathroom and a toilet attached; these two rooms were the domain of the *pani-wallah* (water carrier) and the sweeper, who emptied the "thunder-boxes" and did the most menial of jobs. Compared to the rest of the house, the bathroom was starkly furnished, and contained either a wooden tub, or an oval tin bath, with water stored in large ceramic ali-baba jars; hot water had to be prepared in the yard and brought upstairs under the maid's supervision.

A European household either maintained its own *dhobi-wallah*, who did the laundry, or had it done by professionals. If this essential service was performed by the latter, an unpleasant condition known as dhobi-itch was often encountered, as the clothes were washed in huge communal tanks by the Royal Lakes. Shirts were usually starched with what was known as congee-water (water in which rice had been boiled).

For many of the *memsahibs*, although quality clothes were either acquired from England or at one of the leading departmental stores in Rangoon, a good Indian *dhursi* (tailor) was indispensable and was jealously guarded. Such a treasure was occasionally shared only with the dearest of friends. It was said that the *dhursi* could copy any pattern but that he was incapable of producing an original design.

At night, as the lights were finally extinguished, and the household settled down to sleep, the *durwan* (night watchman) came into his own. Like some shadowy sentinel, he took up his position, armed with a staff and an oil lamp, either by the main gate or under the porch. He was a trusted servant, as many of the houses of the period had no front doors and access would have been remarkably easy for an intruder. Perhaps, because of the presence of the durwan, European houses were rarely visited by burglars, it was the non-Europeans who appear to have been targeted.

Those who had houses in the city complained that the cantonment, which was considered to be more healthy as it was situated on higher ground, had been monopolized by the military. Consequently valuable land had remained undeveloped within its boundary and it was suggested that as a military presence was no longer necessary in Rangoon, the area be turned over to the municipal authorities and the regiments moved to the outskirts further north. The army, which did not always see eye to eye with the civil authorities, dug its heels in and held on to the land until the 1920s.

The Residence of the
Indian Ambassaador,
Ahlone.

Private residence in
Kemmendine.

...a custom-house, handsome stone buildings, hotels, Government offices and streets of shops now greet the traveller's eye on dropping anchor at Rangoon. Beyond the town, and beside broad, well-made roads, are the bungalows of the English, set in the midst of park-like gardens of tamarind, peepul, and palm trees. The beautiful lakes form part of a great public park where gymkhanas delight the gay English residents. Schools and missions are abundant in Rangoon, and here Dr. Marks has carried on his splendid educational work and has educated no less than 15,000 Burmese boys. A large hospital has been established under the care of Dr Johnston and others, and at Lady Dufferin's Fund Hospital the gentle Burmese and Karen women are taught to be nurses of the sick.

Rangoon has become a prosperous British port, but it has not ceased to be Burmese. The Shway Dagohn still dominates the city, and as long as the Burmese youths continue to pass through the portals of the kioungs (monasteries) into manhood, the conquered people will be Buddhist and Burmese to their hearts' core; and for my part I do not wish it otherwise.

MRS HART, PICTURESQUE BURMA, 1897

General Hospital, Rangoon - Nurses' Quarters

The St. Pauls High School, Rangoon

St. John's College -- Rangoon.

In 1895, if one had a dislike of overcrowding, cockroaches, and rats then travelling from India to Burma in a British India steamer, with its characteristic black funnels with two white stripes, was not to be recommended. The company monopolized the lucrative trade route between India and the coastal ports of Burma, and was one of the lines which brought in the immigrants from Madras, 900 miles away; sometimes as many as 3,500 passengers were carried on each small ship. Depending on the weather, it took three to four days from either Calcutta, or Madras.

The Bibby Line which inaugurated regular services from England to Burma in 1891, charged £50, while the Henderson Line a mere £30; the former provided first-class accommodation, while the latter offered only second-class. The journey to the country which was variously referred to as the Land of Dacoits, Fever, Rice, and Rubies, took twenty-five to twenty-eight days. By 1896, it had become fashionable for many of the British inhabitants of Rangoon to say that one always travelled on a Bibby boat, as it was mainly used by the wealthy, and senior government officials. Those who were unable to afford the fare charged by the Bibby, but had pretensions to grandeur, tried to make excuses by complaining that they were forced to use the Henderson, as the line of their first choice had been fully booked. Almost all the ocean-going vessels were now steam-propelled, and it was beginning to be a rare sight to see the old sailing ships.

According to accounts left by European visitors in the 1890s, Rangoon either struck one as highly attractive or instantly unlikable. The city nevertheless had character; apart from the variety of religious places of worship, there were also imposing public buildings, offices, and private dwellings with their diversity of architectural designs. In some residential quarters, a hybridized but exotic effect was produced with the addition of either Burmese, Chinese, or Indian embellishments to the exterior of the more functional European style houses. While some Occidentals thought the pot-pourri of features blended in perfectly with one another, others were appalled.

The broad thoroughfares of the city were busy with pedestrians, among whom were pig-tailed Chinese in traditional costumes; these men were sometimes accompanied by youths in felt hats and Western-style jackets, but wearing loose Chinese trousers. There were also many of the races from India, each in his own distinctive dress; Persians in flowing robes, Malays, Thais, and Indonesians. Occasionally, a group of Burmese could be seen, strolling nonchalantly in their silken clothes down the street. English ladies sat erect in their smart pony-traps or carriages, as they headed for the large departmental stores. On Sundays, long processions of these vehicles could be seen, carrying their smartly dressed occupants to the numerous and varied places of worship. They included Weslyans, Presbyterians, other Protestant denominations, and Roman Catholics.

In the past it had been the custom for European males to dress on informal occasions in white drill suits. This ensemble consisted of a network singlet, a shirt, jacket with a military collar, and a pair of trousers. But by the late 1880s the white suit was being replaced by the latest styles from England, and the men began dressing as they would have done at Home. The reason was that the Eurasian male, or *chi-chi*, who was held in contempt, had also taken to appearing in white. This, of course, could not be tolerated, standards had to be maintained, and a clear visual statement showing the unbridgeable gap between the two had to be put into force. As a result, suits made of thicker materials, and designed for the English climate were adopted. In the sweltering heat of Rangoon, these suits were a disaster, but nevertheless, were worn with a determination for which the British are famous. A number of articles submitted to the *Rangoon Gazette* by members of the medical profession urged the continuation of the wearing of light white suits, yet such advice was studiously ignored.

Among the European mercantile community, there were a number of Germans, who for a few decades, were to compete successfully with the British. Their numbers had been growing steadily, so that by 1867 they found it necessary to open a German Club in Commissioner Road. While few Englishmen, conditioned by their immense sense of superiority, had little or no interest either in the country or the Burmese, many of their German counterparts took the trouble to learn the language. Thus, representatives of the German firms, when negotiating a business deal, were able to enjoy the goodwill of the Burmese merchants in the regions. Like the Chinese, they, too, kept to themselves, and maintained their own church. The German Club was a wooden building, remarkably like a medieval castle with a great central octagonal tower, and looked as if it had been transported from somewhere in the Rhine valley. It was one of the most striking structures in the city, and stood within spacious well-kept grounds.

Almost all the European inhabitants of Rangoon were usually up at sunrise, and after a light *chota-hazri*, or breakfast of tea, toast, and fruit, took the opportunity of either riding or walking in the cool air, for between 11 a.m. and 4 p.m. the heat could become unbearable. After lunch it became the custom for some to have a rest in bed.

Rangoon usually came to life again after tea, when among the younger set, tennis or other games were played, while others took themselves off in their carriages to the Royal Lakes and the scrupulously maintained Dalhousie Park. The latter now covered an area totalling 455 acres, and was enhanced by ornate pavilions and band-stands. It was under the control of the municipality, who claimed that the gardens and views in the park were some of the best in South East Asia. The hoards of Indian gardeners who tended the turf were fortunate in that an endless supply of water was available from the Royal Lakes, with the result that the lawns were always green - a marvel to the Burmese. Many of the groups of carefully planted trees were of such variety that there was a succession of trees in bloom throughout the year.

At a beauty spot variously known as "Scandal Point" or "Gossip Point", the ladies gathered to exchange the latest foreign and local news, while a military band played in the background. The orchid houses which drew large crowds at flowering time could also be enjoyed in the Cantonment Gardens; its principal features were a small lake, a distinctive pavilion in a decadent Burmese style, and an ornamental bridge.

The spectacular setting of the sun behind the Shwedagon signalled to the Indian drivers of the carriages that it was time to collect their *memsahibs* and drive in the direction of either the Gymkhana or the Pegu Club where dances was held every week. The Gymkhana boasted reading rooms, fifteen billiard-tables, including a separate one for the ladies, tennis-courts, and stables. It would seem that one needed extreme patience to play billiards, as the bright lights invariably attracted hordes of flying insects; the surface of the table was often a seething mass. A game had often to be stopped and the lights turned off in the hope that other lights would attract these unwelcome intruders. At the end of a glorious evening the convoys of carriages made their way home under a canopy of brilliant tropical stars, and along streets illuminated by kerosene oil lamps.

During daylight hours, the more adventurous among the Europeans could also explore the area at the foot of Pagoda Hill with its clusters of numerous monasteries. Mrs Hart noted that

Chief Court, Front View — Burma.

"the roofs and balconies of these kioungs or monasteries are handsomely carved. Extending along the roads leading to the pagoda there are long lines of rest-houses, intended for the use of pilgrims who come from a distance to lodge for the night".

New visitors to Rangoon now had a choice of hotels which were under European management. Ideally sited away from the noise of the commercial sector there were two private hotels near the cantonment called Croton Lodge, and Allandale. Here, comfortable accommodation was available at reasonable prices, amidst greenery and tranquillity. In the city, the principal establishments which were situated in the Strand Road were the Oriental, the Great Eastern, Evershed's Hotel and of course the Strand. Being close to the water front their guests enjoyed a refreshing breeze, although the continuous noise from the rail tracks, docks, and the busy river traffic could be trying.

Visitors from the mercantile community usually stayed at Sarkies or Barnes' Family Hotel, both of which were in Merchant Street, the commercial centre of the city. Close by was the Burma Club. The British India, another popular hotel, was conveniently sited in Sule Pagoda Road, with its famous golden shrine on an island in the middle of this long shady avenue. In the 1890s, newly arrived Raj tourists who were driven past this shrine were often told that the Burmese king Alaungmintaya had a Mon prince buried alive beneath it. Although this tale im-

Left: corner tower of the Law Courts Building, opposite Independence Park, formerly Fytch Square.

Next: Burmese religious activities - timeless offerings and prayers.

... to be bewitched by the Shway Dagohn, one must see it by the light of the full moon. It is late, and the moon is high in the heavens as we grope our way in the darkness of the colonnades and stumble up the uneven steps. The wide platform is deserted, not a worshipper disturbs the solitude, not a muttered prayer breaks the silence of the night; the brazen solemn faces of the Gautammas gleam in the shadows, and the Nats on the carved roofs seem to be mutely dancing to the music of the stars. "High striving to the upper air", the tapering capola rises towards the heavens, from which the soughing of the midnight wind wafts down the tinkling of the jewelled bells swinging on the golden htee above. As we descend the hill again to where the monster beasts are staring with blank white faces at the moon, we muse on the mighty power of Buddhism.

MRS HART, PICTURESQUE BURMA, 1897

parted an interesting atmosphere to the shrine, and produced a shudder among the sensitively inclined, it is not mentioned in Burmese or Mon historical accounts, and was an obvious fabrication.

While the city was rapidly emerging as a great commercial centre, at the lower end of the social scale, many of its inhabitants in the outlying sectors were still living in appalling conditions. As late as 1898 the area of Lanmadaw in west Rangoon which contained a large percentage of squatters had become so saturated with filth that it was declared a hazard zone, and parts of the large suburb of Kemmindine had to be abandoned; there were other equally unhealthy sites. Again, because of the lack of funds, very little could be done by the Municipal authorities. Therefore it was not surprising that in the last decade of the nineteenth century, Rangoon suffered several outbreaks of cholera, dysentery, plague, small-pox and typhoid; death rates were high.

Whenever such epidemics occurred in the Burmese quarter, bonfires would be lit in the streets, and the loudest possible noises made with whatever came to hand; this ceremony was called *thayair-mayair* or banishing the demons. People yelled and screamed, and hordes of stray dogs barking or howling in terror added to the commotion. This activity was enthusiastically maintained until the elders decided that the evil spirits which had brought the epidemic had been frightened away. For Europeans new to the country, such an event, which tended to occur without warning, must have been alarming.

In 1898, although a Burma Municipal Act was passed, the changes it brought were superficial. As with the earlier Act of 1884, power remained in the hands of Government which stipulated the number of members on the Committee. The responsibilities of the latter, however, continued to increase.

It has been claimed by a number of modern writers that the Burmese were down-trodden during this period. Yet a visit to the Shwedagon platform would suggest otherwise. Where once the area around the stupa had been relatively free of pavilions and shrines, these now mushroomed in profusion. Many of the older elegant structures, with their superb carvings were dismantled by enthusiastic and pious donors, eager to flaunt their new-found wealth. In their place, garishly decorated buildings, delicately carved pavilions, statuary, and pagodas of modern design jostled for space. Almost all bore the name of its donor, and the cost involved - it being the tradition among Burmese Buddhists to make sure that the general public was informed as to how much was being spent on religion by the donor. Anonymous donations to charity or the discreet commissioning of works of merit are quite alien to the Burmese Buddhist way of thinking.

While the pilgrims converged endlessly onto the great sun-drenched platform and gazed in pious awe at the dazzling sights, quite a few European authors commented on the "depravity of modern Burmese taste" to be found there. Others described the mode of ornamentation "with broken bits of coloured glass and mirrors", as being "in the most garish and depraved manner of Burmese art". One visitor even found the Shwedagon to be "a messy place". Many could not bear the thought of having to walk in bare feet up the filthy stairs, and onto the main platform where beggars and lepers could be found. The universal habit of spitting, which was to be encountered among Orientals, was also most off-putting.

Along the ancient Pilgrim's Way, which was now called Pagoda Road, an imposing public hall to commemorate Queen Victoria's Diamond Jubilee was built on the site of the Assembly Rooms; this was by the old race course. On its completion in 1898, it was admired for the beautifully carved bold panels on the ceiling which were in a Burmese style. It also boasted a sweeping staircase which lead to an impressive gallery. Theatrical performances, grand balls, exhibitions, and receptions were held in the huge ornate interior. Until the late 1930s, the Jubilee Hall was to be the centre of entertainment for the British community.

အရှေ့တိုင်း၏ ကျက်သရေဆောင် ရန်ကုန်ရွှေမြို့တော်

Pearl of the Orient

LIFE IN THE CITY
1900-1919

Three months into the twentieth century, Rangoon society was shocked by the news that one of the English barmaids at Evershed's Hotel had killed herself by taking oxalic acid. There was an immediate outcry from many of the *memsahibs*, clergy, and the Rangoon Christian Temperance Union. The pastor of the Immanuel Baptist Church even petitioned Government to forbid the recruitment of English women for such menial posts, adding that not only was it degrading, but that the prestige of the ruling race was at stake.

The employment of European females in this capacity had begun among the better class of hotels in 1890, and by 1900, at least thirty-six girls were known to have been working in the city. It was pointed out that despite the higher level of remuneration, even the despised Eurasian women avoided taking up such a position. The repercussions were swift. In India, Lord Curzon, the Viceroy, announced that it was unacceptable for European barmaids to be put in the unenviable position of having to serve natives who had the means to patronize these establishments. Despite strong protests from the hotel proprietors of Calcutta, the Bengal Government went ahead with outlawing the continuation of this practice.

Rangoon society was in for yet another shock. News of a more salacious nature concerning the deplorable

BURMAH.

An extensive State in farther India. It is bounded North and West by Assam and Thibet, East by China, South by the Indian Ocean. It is now divided into two kingdoms, British Burmah and Burmah. The climate is quite healthful; the rainy season continues from May to September, following which is a most delightful season until March. In appearance, as our picture indicates, the Burmese are much like the Mongolians, having the same large cheek bones, oblique eyes and short robust figures. The language is similar to the Chinese. Manufactures and agriculture are carried on but indifferently. The principal religion is Buddhism. The Singer Machine was introduced here over 18 years ago, and is extensively used.

THE SINGER MANUFACTURING CO.

Left: shutter-clad façade of a building in Chinatown.

BIBBY LINE

FORTNIGHTLY SAILINGS.
FIRST CLASS PASSENGERS ONLY.

RANGOON, COLOMBO, COCHIN, PORT SAID, PORT SAID,
MARSEILLES, GIBRALTAR, PLYMOUTH, and LONDON.

The fleet consists entirely of Twin Screw Vessels, all fitted with bilge keels and specially built for the First Class Eastern Passenger Trade.

"Derbyshire" *	.. Tons Capacity	.. 15,000		"Yorkshire"	.. Tons Capacity	.. 13,500
" Worcestershire " *	.. Tons Capacity	.. 15,000		"Lancashire "	.. Tons Capacity	.. 13,000
"Staffordshire " *	.. Tons Capacity	.. 15,000		"Oxfordshire "	.. Tons Capacity	.. 12,500
"Shropshire " *	.. Tons Capacity	.. 15,000		"Somersetshire " *	.. Tons Capacity	.. 10,500
" Cheshire " *	.. Tons Capacity	.. 15,000		"Dorsetshire " *	.. Tons Capacity	.. 10,500

* Motor Vessels

AGENTS :

RANGOON · Steel Brothers & Co., Ltd.
SINGAPORE
and PENANG Paterson, Simons & Co., Ltd.
BANGKOK · The Anglo-Siam Corporation, Ltd.
MARSEILLES · Watson, Browne & Co., 5a, Rue Beauvau.

COLOMBO - - - - Carson & Co., Ltd.
COCHIN - - - Harrisons & Crosfield, Ltd.
PORT SUDAN - - - Gellatly, Hankey & Co.
:Sudan: Ltd
SUEZ and PORT SAID · Wm. Stapledon & Sons.

BIBBY BROS. & CO., Martins Bank Building, Water St., Liverpool ; 22, Pall Mall, London, S.W.1.

morals of two barmaids now spread like wildfire. It was said that the pair had become so debauched that one of them, a Miss Matherson, had openly taken to soliciting coolies in the seedy liquor shops. At the time, the coolies who were encountered in the streets of Rangoon were mainly Coringhi, coarse and illiterate natives of India. They were generally considered to be the lowest of the low, not only by the British, but also by the Burmese and the Indians. This particular scandal utterly devastated the prim Victorian ladies who gathered within the exclusive portals of the Gymkhana, and the Pegu Clubs; the final fate of Miss Matherson is not known.

Following the scandal over the barmaids, the thorny question of British officials keeping Burmese mistresses was again enthusiastically revived by those who considered themselves guardians of public morals. A Mrs Ada Castle, the wife of an officer in the Burma Police, wrote to Curzon, declaring that she was about to launch a campaign against immorality in the province. Among the "disgraceful" cases she cited, was that of an official called Minns, who was soon to become the Deputy Commissioner of Rangoon, and who was openly keeping two Burmese mistresses. The Castle woman made such a nuisance of herself, that it was remarked that she was the type of person who was quite capable of finding fornicators lurking even within the Pearly Gates.

Earlier, the *Sudhakar*, a newspaper in Bengal had protested at the heartless way in which English officials were debauching Burmese women. To be fair to these 'debauchers', it must be pointed out that no one was dragged kicking and screaming into a relationship. On the contrary, as mentioned earlier, an Englishmen was considered quite a catch. Among the Burmese, unattached men and women - unless religiously motivated - have always been an enigma, and it was the most natural thing to find a partner. To quote an example, as early as 1638, a royal order by Thalun (r.1629-48) was circulated instructing the elders of his kingdom that youths and maidens, widows and widowers, should not remain single, and were to be encouraged to marry as soon as possible. It would seem that such concern for connubial bliss extended even to foreign prisoners of war, who were invariably provided with Burmese wives.

The result of all this interference with the private lives of even the most senior officials had a detrimental effect on their careers. Promotions were denied, and there was talk of either a transfer to India, or even dismissal. Despite the attitude of the Government, several Englishmen took the plunge and married their mistresses. This action effectively cut them off from many of the social gatherings at which the *burra memsahib* - a formidable and elevated being - presided.

Dautrimer, the French Consul in Rangoon, said that among the British in India, a rigid caste system existed. As Burma was considered a mere extension of that country, government administrators and their wives who arrived to take up new posts in Rangoon behaved in exactly the same way they would have done in India. Dautrimer, who was ideally placed to observe this social phenomenon said he found it "almost comical".

In Burma, the European male was called *thakin*, and a female *thakinma*, and not *sahib*, or *memsahib*, as in India. Although Maung Htin Aung in *The History of Burma* claimed that the term *thakin* came into use sometime in 1886, Trant, in his *Two Years in Ava*, said that in 1825 "many little songs, amongst others that commencing "Tekien, Tekien" [*thakin*] were composed and sung by the Burman fair in compliment to their new and welcome visitors, the white strangers".

According to Dautrimer, at the very apex of Rangoon society were the august personages from the Indian Civil Service, who were referred to as the "heaven-born" by their envious underlings. Although the art of being 'charming' was effortlessly practiced, the inferior recipient always had to remember not to step out of line and become familiar. Such graciousness was expected to be received gratefully.

Privately, this small group of dignitaries circulated only within their own tightly-knit circle, and "did not deign to go outside their caste to widen their acquaintance". Englishmen and women of such exalted rank had "scarcely more than an eye-acquaintance with the

From **Rangoon** *to*
Port Sudan, Port Said, Marseilles, London, Liverpool and **Glasgow**
AND OTHER UNITED KINGDOM AND CONTINENTAL PORTS

AGENCY :
RANGOON : Steel Bros. & Company, Limited.
FOR PASSENGER ENQUIRIES ONLY
RANGOON —Thos. Cook & Son Ltd.   PENANG :—Paterson Simons & Co., Ltd.
RANGOON —A. Scott & Co.   SINGAPORE :—Paterson Simons & Co., Ltd.
HEAD OFFICE:
P. HENDERSON & Co.,
95, Bothwell Street, GLASGOW, C. 2 and at 48 50, St. Mary Axe, LONDON, E.C. 3.

son of the soil". Cocooned in a small and insular world, such people felt duty bound to maintain British power and exclusiveness at all costs.

For a time, even high-ranking British military officers and their wives were rarely invited to tea. This was not surprising, for it was said that the military did not get on with their civilian compatriots, and kept to their cantonment, socialising in their regimental clubs. The same attitude was to be witnessed among the British junior administrators, merchant classes, and other groups. It was only on high days and state occasions, that these people would come together on the spacious lawns of Government House. Even then, many kept to their own circle, and for a time, "everyone knew their place".

Dautrimer noted that almost all the English residents in Burma were friendly to "foreigners" [Europeans], provided, of course, certain social rules were strictly observed. This condescension, however, does not appear to have been extended to non-Europeans. Some of those who were foolish enough to invite wealthy and educated "Orientals" to a dinner party were soon taught a sharp lesson. On sweeping into the drawing room, a grand *burra memsahib* would stare at such guests, as if in utter bewilderment and surprise, and demand to know who on earth these extraordinary people were. The implication was crystal clear - her fellow guests were totally out of place, and should not have been there; the atmosphere in the room for the remainder of the evening can well be imagined.

It was noticed, even in later years, that while beyond the confines of Rangoon the British and Burmese often enjoyed a cordial relationship, within the city the attitude of many of the former was one of a chill reserve and formality.

At the turn of the century the Land of the Golden Pagodas and Fair Ladies could be reached by

... the place lacks the colour and cleanness of Colombo; it is untidy, unfinished, a town in the making. There are great imposing buildings it is true, but they are set amid small mean hovels and waste places covered with lumber. The crowd is cosmopolitan, not by any means Burmese, and the general effect is bewildering.

G E MITTON, BACHELOR GIRL IN BURMA, 1907

embarking from either Glasgow, or Liverpool, on one of the comfortable steamers of the Bibby or the Henderson Lines. The return fare, valid for two years, on the Bibby boats had now increased to £75.

Many avoided the monsoons, as it usually rained for days, and could be very unpleasant. The damp encouraged mould to grow, rapidly covering books, furniture and clothing, and leaving an unpleasant odour. The best time to visit the country was between November and February, although it was warm during the day, the nights could be cool, and occasionally become chilly towards morning. There was neither rain nor excessive heat, and excursions into the interior could be enjoyable.

After landing at the Sule Pagoda Wharf, the agents of Thomas Cook provided all that was essential for a reasonably comfortable trip. This included bedding, utensils, tinned food, and most vital of all, an Indian servant who could speak English and Burmese. The agents for Thomas Cook usually had a busy time between November and February due to the rush of globe-trotters eager to 'do' the country.

From the capital, access into the interior could either be on one of the Irrawaddy Flotilla steamers, or by Burma Railways. If travelling by rail, the first class carriages were comfortable, with small folding tables, and seats which could be turned into sleeping berths. Each carriage had its own lavatory. Some trains had special 'market carriages', a veritable shop on wheels which brought foreign goods to out of the way stations. Some of the larger towns along the way even catered for the European trade with well organised restaurants.

A more adventurous tourist could kit himself out at Barnett Brothers with a light fold-away bed, table, chairs, and tinned food, while tropical wear, mosquito net, and bedding could be acquired from Rowe and Company; both these firms were conveniently sited in Fytche Square.

Other shops owned by Burmans, Europeans, and Indians, specialized in curios and other items dear to the hearts of foreign residents and visitors alike. At the time, the three leading companies were Beato, Watts and Skein, and Goomanal Parasram. Burmese-owned shops were all located in Godwin Road, where delicately carved objects of ivory and wood were available. As many of the master craftsmen from the interior had decided to settle in Rangoon, the city soon became famous for works of art in these two materials.

Some tourists, however, had neither the time nor the inclination to travel and remained in Rangoon, staying at one of its numerous hotels. There were also boarding houses and smaller private establishments, the latter were to be found in the cantonment, and were managed mainly by the widows of European officers.

One visitor remarked that the hotels in the city should be of interest to the naturalist, as a variety of insects, lizards, striped squirrels, and muskrats could be encountered in one's bedroom. Another complained that although most rooms had telephones, they rarely worked, and when they did, there was really nothing in the hotel worth asking for.

On the other hand, the artist, Talbot Kelly, who stayed at the Strand Hotel was delighted to find that his well furnished bedroom had a verandah. However, he was rather surprised to see that apart from the mosquito net, mattress, and pillow, there was no other bed linen - apparently this was the only way to sleep during the hot season. Another visitor praised the hotel for its incomparable omelette, claiming that it was the only thing which made it worth while to visit the city.

A visitor 'doing' the city, would have found that the government and public buildings were large and impressive, and dominated the skyline; the most conspicuous being the extremely ornate Post Office in the Strand Road. While some had architectural merit, others were simply copies of structures to be seen in the West and the Middle East. Earlier, strong criticism in the local press had followed the completion of some of these buildings. One critic went so far as to say that the design of the Law Courts was possibly the work of a convict who had a grudge against his Judge.

By 1905, the building of the Secretariat which had begun in 1890, was completed; the archi-

The kitchens at the Strand Hotel, 1930s.

tecture was wittily referred to as "bureaucratic Byzantine". It was a huge complex, dominated by a large dome, reminiscent of the Florence Duomo. Its vast number of rooms contained various departments, all of which looked out onto well maintained gardens and tennis courts which were open to the public after office hours.

The worst time to see Rangoon was at the end of the monsoon season. By then, because of the incessant rains, all the houses were usually discoloured by dark stains, and green moss-like growths. Talbot Kelly thought that Rangoon, with its excellent wharfs and warehouses, was a "handsome city", and was impressed with its magnificent river. As the docks swarmed with coolies from Chittagong and Madras, Kelly's first impression of Rangoon was that he had arrived at a city in India. He noted that burly Sikh police constables kept a watchful eye on the pedestrians and the traffic and saluted on sight only Europeans. These men, who were chosen for their height and build, wore black woollen tunics and sweltered in the heat, yet they were always smartly turned out.

As an artist, Kelly saw the city in a different light. With its multi-cultural inhabitants, entertainments, religious processions, and places of worship, everything seemed conveniently concentrated within a radius of fifteen square miles. In particular, he found the drive out of the city to the European residential area enjoyable. He noticed that all the roads, which were wide and well maintained, were shaded by exotic trees, and that the private gardens were stocked with native and other plants brought back from England. The wooden houses and bungalows, some of which were covered in climbing plants, were spacious and well designed, indicating the prosperity of their owners.

Observing that the Burmese still kept to their own quarters on the outskirts of the city, Kelly noted that they were only visible in central Rangoon when they came on shopping sprees, or to pray at the Sule, and the Botataung pagodas. At the latter, many devout Buddhists were offended by the graves of the British soldiers who had died during the 1852 Second Anglo-Burmese War and which were still to be seen near the sacred platform; among them was the grave of the Rev. Thomas Baker, author of *Recent Operations of the British Forces at Rangoon and Martaban*. The

STRAND SH HOTEL
RANGOON

MENU
DINER

1. Hors d'Oeuvres Varies

2. Consomme Double Royal

3. Creme Longchamps

4. Supremes de Bectie Mornay

5. Caneton Sauvage en Cocotte
Petits Pois & Carotes Clamard
Pommes Noisette

6. Cromesky Polonaise

7. Quartier d'Agneau Roti Sce Menthe
Chouxfleurs au Beurre
Pommes Mirette

8 Meringues Glacees

Dessert

Cafe

Tuesday 6th December 1932.

Guest Nights.

There will be music in the hotel, and Dancing in the Strand Hall after dinner, every Wednesday night when the "Harmonists" orchestra will play for residents, guests, and visitors.

Telegraphic Address: "STRANDHO," RANGOON.
Telegraphic Code Words :

IJAAW = Please reserve (one) single bedroom (without private bathroom attached) in the Annexe.
IJFIO = Please reserve (one) single bedroom (without private bathroom attached) in the main building.
IJKNE = Please reserve (one) single bedroom (with private bathroom attached) in the main building.
IJOTS = Please reserve (one) double bedroom (without private bathroom attached) in the main building.
IJUPZ = Please reserve (one) double bedroom (with private bathroom attached) in the main building.
IUMLA = Please reserve one sitting room.

If more than one bedroom is required, add one of the following codewords **after** one of the foregoing codewords.

VAPBA	= 2	VAUBI	= 5	VHATO	= 8
VARKL	= 3	VEYJY	= 6	VHEVZ	= 9
VASPT	= 4	VEZIZ	= 7	VHIWI	= 10

NOTE.—Two words can be joined together and sent as one word.

EXAMPLES.

(1). IJUPZVARKL = Please reserve three double bedrooms (with private bathrooms attached) in the main building.

(2). IJOTSIJAAW = Please reserve one double bedroom (without private bathroom attached) in the main building and one single bedroom (without private bathroom attached) in the Annexe.

(3). IJKNEVAPBA IJAAW = Please reserve two single bedrooms (with private bathrooms attached) in the main building and one single bedroom (without private bathroom attached) in the Annexe.

The Code words used in this Brochure are taken from the A.B.C. Code 6th Edition by permission of the Proprietors. Codes used A.B.C. 6th Edition and Bentley's.

map of 1852 indicates that there was a military hospital near the site. It should be noted that the Christian custom of using a churchyard as a cemetery is an idea totally alien to the Burmese; cemeteries are considered to be unclean and the domain of evil spirits and are sited well away from human habitation.

Kelly also visited the picturesque village of Wingaba (labyrinth) set in acres of shady trees, from the tops of which the carved spires of numerous monasteries pierced the sky. In the centre was a sacred lake which was bordered by shrubs, prayer halls and rest houses for pilgrims; the structures were built on piles so that the verandahs jutted out over the lotus strewn surface.

Wingaba was also well known for an enormous reclining figure of the Buddha, called the U Po Tha Phaya, after its wealthy donor who was later knighted. Images in this posture indicate that the sage is about to depart this world and enter Nivarna, and are appropriately shown with the

Shrines at Wingaba Pagoda

head resting either on one palm or pillows. This figure, on the other hand, was the handiwork of an incompetent Indian whose knowledge of sculpture and Burmese culture were non-existent. Built up of layers of bricks, the clumsily moulded and ugly face, with a broad frog-like mouth and elongated body, gave it a nightmarish quality. Contrary to the traditional posture, this image was depicted propped up on one elbow, and rearing its monstrous head high above the treetops.

Among the more tranquil settings, in another Burmese quarter were the Buddhist monasteries which were to be found around the base of the Shwedagon. Of these, the two most famous were the Shwegyin Monastery which was built by Mindon Min in 1867, and the impressive Taing-taya Kyaung (Monastery of the One Hundred Pillars). There were other less imposing structures in Kemmindine and Pazundaung, with many dating only from the second half of the nineteenth century.

Kelly thought that one example which illustrated the difference in outlook between the Burmese and the races of India, was the way in which each treated their beasts of burden. Whilst the Indians cruelly overworked and abused their animals, the Buddhist Burmese cared for them. Kelly concluded that this innate gentleness hardly equipped the Burman "to compete with the aggressive and noisy cupidity of others, whose one aim would seem to be to extract as much as possible from either man or beast".

The artist had been told that Burmese men were inclined to laziness, while the women were energetic in business matters. Nevertheless, his opinion was that "even if the Burman is somewhat indolent and conceited, his indolence is largely that of the gentleman of leisure, while so much of grace and beauty envelops the concept that we readily forgive it".

By the early 1900s, the Burmese had become so used to the presence of Europeans that the lower classes were no longer prepared to *shikho* (kneeling with both palms raised and bowing to the ground) every European they met. Kelly said that "one of the unfortunate effects of our occu-

Wingaba Lakes, Rangoon.

pation of Burma has been the gradual undermining of this ancient courtesy, and in Rangoon is almost a thing of the past". During those halcyon Imperial days, such was the ingrained British sense of superiority, or for that matter most Europeans, that they rather peevishly complained that while all the other native races respectfully *salaam* the white man "the Burman alone declines to *shikho* to any one, passing by with an air of unconscious indifference".

Although the educated young Burmese males in Rangoon still wore their national costume, which consisted of a shirt, long sleeved jacket, and silk *pasoe* (sarong), they had replaced the two-thonged slippers with patent-leather shoes and silk socks. The traditional *gaung-baung* (turban) could now only be seen on older men, and government officials, as it was no longer fashionable among the young who had taken to cutting their hair in the European style. Also discarded were the 'whacking great cheroots', about a foot long, which were considered too 'provincial'; American cigarettes, and slim cigars were thought to be more suitable for a young man about town.

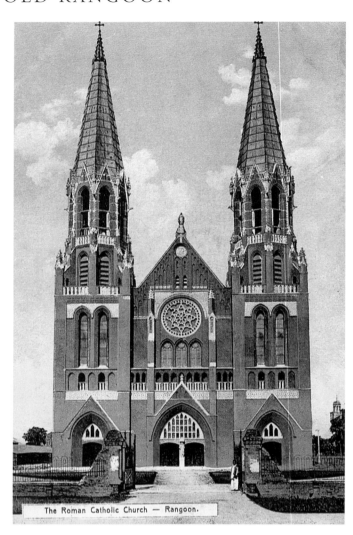

The Roman Catholic Church — Rangoon.

Throughout the country, it was soon accepted among the Burmese that anything new, either in the world of the arts, or fashion, had its origins in cosmopolitan Rangoon. Although it must be said that unlike some members of the elite classes from other emerging Asian countries, European suits were rarely worn even by the most westernized of Burmese men. Likewise, Burmese women would have found it hysterically funny to see one of their race in a Western dress. They preferred to wear their traditional costume, artfully modified to suit modern tastes which in the process somehow emphasised their delicate femininity.

Visting European men, after experiences in India, were quick to notice the difference in demeanour between the women of that country and those of Burma. On encountering a European, the former drew her sari across her face and looked away, while the latter looked him straight in the eye without any compunction.

Whether at home, or in public, the younger ladies from among the better classes were always carefully made up, with jewellery and flowers in their hair. When visiting either the pagoda or paying social calls, a long *pawa* (scarf) of the finest silk was casually draped across the shoulders, and allowed to float about her as she walked. Is is little wonder that quite a few Englishmen cast covetous eyes in the direction of these "pretty creatures". In the inevitable encounters, while the fortunate ones, and they were few, enjoyed marriage to an Englishman, others were relegated to the half-world of the kept woman.

The author, Mitton, a somewhat severe looking lady, who was later to become the wife of George Scott, was not impressed with the Burmese beauties. She wrote in *A Bachelor Girl in Burma* that "my visit dissipated finally the idea of the Burman girls being "pretty" according to our ideas. They are sometimes dear coquettish little things with a great deal of charm and some personality, but to apply the word "pretty" to their broad noses, flat little faces, thanaka-stained, and the straight greased hair, is a misuse of adjectives". She concluded that they were certainly "taking, charming, gracious, and alluring; but not pretty." Scott had once described Burmese and Japanese women as having "the power of beauty without the possession of it". Judging by the Eurasian communities throughout the country, it would seem that a large number of Englishmen did not agree, and were absolutely captivated by the "dainty little beauties".

As new areas in Rangoon were reclaimed and opened up, the population increased. Added to the numerous problems was the predictable one of water supply. The Kokine reservoir had by now become inadequate for the increasing number of city dwellers and by 1901 could no longer be relied on. Eventually a large reservoir at Hlawga was constructed, and opened in 1904. Due to mismanagement in its construction even this new source was to have its troubles.

Other familiar problems for the city were abductions, murders, and robberies. This was due to an insufficient number of police. There were also outbreaks of gang warfare in the Indian community, the two leading villains being Meshidi and Mamsa who fought each other for supremacy

Religious and ethnic diversity in Old Rangoon: a Chinese church in Ahlone and detail of the Indian mosque ajacent to the Sule Pagoda, Downtown.

Rangoon Harbour.   No. 5

Barr Street Jetty, Rangoon.

Left and top right: the Sule Pagoda from the air and from Fytche Square.

၁၉၃၀ ခုနှစ်လောက်တွင်ရိုက်ကူ ထာ သော ဆူ လေဘုရာ လမ်

Above: Sule Pagoda Road in the 1930s.

[the city was] ...past redemption by any sort of beauty, and must go the way it is rapidly taking towards a turgid and indiscriminate prosperity. ... an amorphous mess of hovels, mansions, half-way houses, spread out over eight square miles of mud at the meeting place of two rivers... scarcely one of its ugly rectangular roads in which some building is not rising higher than all the rest, but not one with the saving grace of the least hint of style, mere stupid ostentatious accumulation of masonry, expressing nothing but the money in them.

PREVOST BATTERSBY
INDIA UNDER ROYAL EYES, 1906.

Burmese and Karen fruit sellers. *The Graphic,* November 14, 1885.

in the drugs, prostitution, and protection rackets. Fights were common between their henchmen, who are said to have terrorised parts of Rangoon. The malevolent shadows of these two criminals probably fell only on the non-European communities. Despite the newspaper reports, it is doubtful if any of the Europeans felt themselves in any danger, as their lives were lived on a totally different level. Although there was a police presence in the city, many of the badly paid constables were usually bought off with bribes.

The secret societies of the Chinese were also another headache for the authorities. Their members struck such terror among their own people that many dared not report the injustices perpetrated on them. But despite its darker side which rarely touched an outsider, the Chinese quarter outwardly presented a bright and cheerful appearance. China Town could boast many finely built residential houses in the traditional style. Those of the rich merchants had lavish interiors with furniture and objets d'art imported from China and the Straits Settlements. The exquisitely carved wood panels which divided the rooms were usually painted red - an auspicious and lucky colour. If one were invited to enter, there was nothing within to indicate that the house was anywhere but in China. Almost all the buildings were constructed with the main door in the middle, as it was believed that good fortune only entered from the centre.

Rangoon's main Chinese communities were divided into two groups. Those who originated from Canton, and those who arrived from Fukien; a good natured rivalry is said to have existed between them. The Burmese referred to the former as *eingyi-toe* (short jackets) and the latter as *eingyi-shay* (long jackets), after their distinctive costumes. The Cantonese who were mainly artisans had to keep their hands unhampered by long sleeves and a long coat, while the Fukienese being of the leisurely merchant class wore the more formal ankle-length robe.

It is believed that there was already a small temple servicing this community from as early as the latter half of the eighteenth century. One of the more resplendent shrines in the area was the Cantonese Temple, the site is also the oldest, since it appeared on a map of the town which is dated 1853. The original temple, which was of timber, had been burnt down in 1855, and although a temporary hall was erected, it was decided to build a brick structure in 1864, with annexes being added in 1872. These impressive buildings were ornamented with superb decorations, including multi-hued ceramic figures. The hall and chambers within blazed with gold leaf and were lit by red lanterns. All the materials for the entire building had been laboriously shipped from China and assembled by the finest craftsmen.

The equally opulent Fukienese Temple was appropriately sited close to the Rangoon River, from the use of which their merchants and junk-owners derived much of their wealth. The foundations were laid in 1861, and the temple, which was of intricately carved wood, was dedicated in 1863. The present magnificent brick structure was only erected in 1903. Further to the north at Kokine, and set in rural surroundings, was another temple called the Ju-shan, which was also built by members of the prosperous Fukienese community in January 1875.

As the Chinese are by nature tolerant, the grounds of both the temples in town were usually filled with people of many races, either sightseeing or making business transactions in some quiet corner; Indian fishermen were sometimes to be observed repairing their nets in the courtyard. Such a casual attitude was not encouraged in the mosques and Hindu temples of the city.

The long standing presence of the Chinese in Rangoon is indicated by a large burial ground reserved for them which can be seen in a map of 1824. In later years, the St. Mary's Cathedral of the Holy Trinity was allotted this prime site, and the cemetery moved to the suburbs by the British, against the wishes of the Chinese.

In Rangoon, as far as public transport was concerned, its citizens still relied on the tram, and horse-drawn vehicles called *tikka gharries*. The **gharry** was a small box-like cab on four iron-tyred wheels, which was driven by a *gharry wallah* (driver) who sat with his assistant in front and at roof level. Neither of the men could speak English, which made it very trying for tourists and residents who had no knowledge of Hindustani. It cost twelve annas for the first hour, and eight for the next. A ride in one, with its hard wooden seats, was described by many to have been "indescribably uncomfortable".

On a higher scale were the smart victorias and landaus, but these were said to have been very expensive. Almost all the European residents had their own carriages, pony-traps and dog-carts; the latter two were sometimes known as *tum-tums*.

In the Burmese quarters, the two-wheeled bullock carts, called *hle-yin* (dainty cart) and *hle*, were common; the former which was of a lighter construction, was beautifully carved, with upward sweeping rail-guards, and was used for social occasions, while the latter was a sturdier contraption and was employed either for travel, or the carrying of heavy merchandise. Among the upper class Burmese and civil servants, European carriages were used.

The streets of Rangoon were soon to see changes, and in 1905 the first motor car appeared and caused a sensation. But soon they were a common sight, and were being driven by anyone who could afford them. The motor car became so popular that the authorities were forced to pass the Burma Motor Vehicles Act in 1906.

Another sensation in 1905 was the third documented poltergeist manifestation in the city. This time the unhappy victim was U Hmaing (Mr Gloomy), who lived in Crisp Street. Stones were thrown or dropped from the ceiling in front of amazed onlookers, many of whom were hit. The phenomenon which predictably drew large crowds, was reported to have continued for a fortnight until a service was held by a magician-monk from Moulmein.

In January 1906, Burma was graced by another royal visit. The by now familiar routine was followed in Rangoon, and the usual garishly ornate triumphal arches appeared along the route to Government House, occupied at the time by the Lieutenant-Governor and Lady Thirkell White. At the wharf, over two thousand people were crowded in the reception area to welcome the Prince and Princess of Wales, later to be crowned King George V and Queen Mary. Among the leading members of the various communities were the Shan Chiefs, dressed in their golden robes of state. It was noticed that the Burmese dignitaries were placed in an annex to the main pavilion. As the royal couple passed through on their way to the state carriage, rose petals from silver bowls were scattered in their path by silk clad and bejewelled Burmese maidens.

The usual round of tours and entertainments followed. One such event included a display of dances by the "wild tribes", which were performed on the vast lawn of Government House. A guest remarked, rather unkindly, that "this inane performance was carried out with a gravity comical in its intensity".

It would seem that the appearance of Rangoon did not meet with the approval of two of the authors who accompanied the royal party. Prevost Battersby, in his *India Under Royal Eyes* was less than kind in his remarks about Rangoon whilst Stanley Reed, who recorded *The Royal Tour in India*, noted that "each good building alternates with hovels, and although Rangoon is a city of infinite promise, it is of the most featureless and unprepossessing achievement. This is Burma without the Burmans, who are the scarcest commodity in Rangoon".

Reed went on to say that the Burman in his own land was:

> ... jostled by Sikh policemen and Indian soldiers. In the buzzing market he is elbowed aside by Chinese, Mussulman and Hindu traders. If he embarks on any enterprise you may be sure that the capital is found by a Madras Chetty or a Chinese money-lender, and that but a meagre share of the profits finds its way into Burmese cash-boxes.

Reed was informed that year by year the Burman fell more deeply into the toils of the Madras and Chinese money-lender, and that the term "native" was never applied to the children of the soil, but to the alien immigrants from India. He felt concerned enough to ask "are we going to wait till the Burman has been squeezed so tight that the process of saving him has become doubly difficult, if not impossible?" Indeed, so large was the Indian community in Rangoon that Hindustani was the common language used by Europeans when dealing with their servants, or when they were in the native quarter.

In 1906, there were 80,000 Burmese in Rangoon, but it was said that "they have little to do with the life of the city". This curious situation appears to have been confined to Rangoon only, and was to continue into the next decade; in other parts of the country it was a different story, and Burmese rupee millionaires were not unknown.

As 1906 came to a close, the first electric tramcar was introduced by the Rangoon Electric Tramway and Supply Company, and by the following year had replaced the old steam versions. Although many of the drivers were Europeans, a ride on a tram was still studiously avoided by the British. The same company was also responsible in 1907 for using electricity to illuminate the streets, which were now constantly busy from well before dawn until late into the night. And for the first time, electric lights were also used to illuminate the Sule Pagoda.

For the Burmese, one of the most novel of sights in the city was the Zoological Gardens, which had been enlarged and reopened in 1906 by the Prince and Princess of Wales. Until 1910, the prize exhibit was the White Elephant, a rather unhealthy looking beast, and one of a surviving pair which had lorded it within the royal palace at Mandalay. The acres of well-kept gardens contained cages of mainly birds, reptiles, and other wild animals indigenous to the country; the entrance fee was one pice. Within its grounds was a statue of Sir Arthur Phayre, Chief Commissioner of Burma between 1862 and 1867, whose *History of Burma*, the earliest work of its kind, was published in 1883. This was the first Western cast bronze statue in Rangoon and it now stands before Belwood, the residence of the British Ambassador.

By 1910, the old Town Hall which was sited close to the Sule Pagoda, had become so dilapidated and infested with plague-infected rats that it had to be demolished. The following year, plans were put in hand for the erection of a large and more appropriate building, but work was held up by the onset of the First World War.

The first decade of the nineteenth century ended with a Burmese Arts and Crafts Exhibition. Among the exhibits the objects which appealed to most Europeans were the ornate silver items, which were produced by master craftsmen such as Maung Yin Maung and other leading silversmiths who had their workshops in Godwin Road.

By 1911, a new General hospital had replaced the old one, which was of timber and totally inadequate for the burgeoning population of Rangoon. It was a huge masonry complex set within landscaped gardens and erected on the site previously occupied by the Agri-Horticultural Society and the Phayre Museum. The architect who designed the nurses' quarters appeared to have been influenced by the Renaissance style, as the building could easily have blended into any suburb in Rome.

Many of the imposing civil and government buildings which were to survive into the 1970s, and which were to become a feature of Rangoon had either been built, or were in the process of being completed. Although contemporary photographs verify that parts of the city were capable of possessing a certain grandeur, in 1912, the author Maurice Collis described the appearance of Rangoon as being rather "shabby".

Thirkell White, writing in 1913, commented on the way Rangoon was changing, and complained about the large number of closely packed dwellings of a "decadent type" which were springing up, and which had "devastated" the once picturesque cantonment. He was shocked to

As you walk along the street
Many curious folk you meet,
Nearly every sort of man
From the shores of Hindustan;
Persians, Turks, and bland Parsis,
Moguls, Gurkhas, Siamese,
Placid folk from far Cathay -
Where's the Burman stowed away?

RODWAY SWINHOE,
THE INCOMPLETE
GUIDE TO BURMA, C.1923.

find that "natives of wealth and position" were now living in areas which were once reserved for the sovereign race.

In 1911 the tram company put into service five motor-buses, and within two years increased the number to eight. In competition were twenty-eight taxi cabs, weaving through the thick traffic of motor cars, trams, hand-carts, bullock carts, and horse drawn *gharries*. By 1915, the number of privately owned cars and lorries had soared to 426. There were also 139 motor cycles, which were said to be a menace in the crowded streets. The enormous increase in traffic had a devasting effect on the roads, causing the macadamised surfaces to crumble. Many of the buildings along the bus lanes were also being affected by the vibrations caused by these vehicles.

Fortunately, escape was still possible from the noise and pressures of the city in any one of the public parks. In the evening Gossip Point on the Royal Lakes was a popular choice as Rangoon society tended to congregate there "in all descriptions of wheeled vehicles". For many of the ruling race it was important to be seen at the right places at the right times, and the *memsahibs* who once rode in their carriages with the *syce* holding an umbrella over them, now glided by in their motor cars. The age-old routine was still followed, in which after a pleasant drive along the red laterite road which ringed Dalhousie Park, they were taken either to the Gymkhana or the Pegu Club, or to a social gathering at the home of some senior civil servant or wealthy merchant.

The European ladies had quite a selection of sports to choose from. There was badminton,

Edwardian tourists visit a Buddhist shrine. Note that they are disrespectfully wearing shoes, an act which Burmese Buddhists find extremely offensive.

ဘုရား လည် ဖူ ရင်
လိပ်ပြ လည် တု ရင်

croquet, tennis, riding, fishing, and for those who were more energetic, exciting but exhausting shooting trips with their partners. Among the younger set, amateur theatricals were all the rage. The affordable Box Brownie camera, first introduced in 1900, had become an indispensable accessory on any outing and pictures of the "quaint little natives" in their curious costumes "simply had to be taken". During the cool season, when the number of Europeans in the city tended to be at its highest, the round of social events increased. At the time, the latest entertainment from England and Europe could be enjoyed at the Jubilee Hall.

Fytche Square, in central Rangoon, had matured and had turned into an extremely picturesque green oasis ringed by offices, shops, and banks, and dominated by the gilded spire of the Sule Pagoda. Within the grounds, and close by the pavilion, a white marble statue of Queen Victoria now gazed imperiously from her plinth in the direction of the Town Hall and the pagoda.

On the increasingly busy waterfront, the treacherous currents of the capricious Rangoon River had begun to erode areas of the bank, threatening the destruction of many fine wharves. It was therefore decided that a retaining wall two miles long be built, and on its completion in 1914, work on much needed improvements along this stretch were put in hand, making the port one of the finest in the East.

Throughout the country, a large majority of the Burmese continued to accept Brtish rule, as many firmly believed that the Government had their prosperity at heart. But such misplaced beliefs were soon shattered as their politically aware and better informed compatriots in Rangoon began to point out that Burma was only a province of India, and that it took second place in the scheme of things. These nationalists were only too aware that as far as the Government was concerned, the wealth of the country was there to be syphoned off, with very little left to benefit the

Left: **The Viceroy inspecting a guard of honour at the new Town Hall, 1937.**

အင်္ဂလိပ်ဘုရင်ခံရန်ကုန်မြို့တော်ခမ်းမကြီးသို့လာစည်၊ ၁၉၃၇ ခုနှစ်

Right: **Sule Pagoda Road in the 1930s.**

၁၉၃၀ခုနှစ်လောက်တွင်ရိုက်ကူးထားသောဆူးလေဘုရားလမ်း

Next left: remnants of the once comonplace wooden architecture of Old Rangoon - monastic and residential; *right:* portals to a private residence on Fraser (Taw-win) Road.

181

Burmese. Among the educated middle and upper classes, many began to question the attitude of the Government and in emulation of their Indian counterparts small political organisations began to be formed.

The move towards self-government had first begun to be put into force, albeit in a cautious fashion, as early as 1897, but it was a lengthy process. Any progress was effectively being retarded by a powerful clique of the old guard among the senior civil servants of the Government of India. Nevertheless, on the face of it, gradual changes were on the way. Although a Legislative Council for Burma was established, it was composed of members who were nominated and not elected, so they had no power. Firm control, including finance, was still exercised by the Government in India.

Meanwhile, adverse conditions in Europe soon culminated in the First World War of 1914-18. This was to have an detrimental effect on Burma, with trade being seriously damaged. Many of the Austrian and German businesses were forced to close. Although their departure signalled a downward spiral in the teak trade, it also meant that desirable residential property came onto the Rangoon market; this was eagerly snapped up by speculators. Also closed was the large brooding building which housed the German Club, its huge hall no longer resounded to the merry drinking songs of its members. The site was acquired by a religious order and a convent built.

The German-owned rice mills along the Rangoon River were also sold off to English companies by the Liquidator of Hostile Firms. But despite having the competition removed, many established British and Indian firms also went out of business. To make matters worse, the presence of the *Emden*, a formidable German warship, which was lurking in the Bay of Bengal, effectively scared off shipping from the busy sea lanes, and in particular the port of Rangoon.

Admidst alarming rumours which were beginning to effect the citizens, the Indian coolies who worked on the docks decided to go on strike, but were quickly brought to heel by a pay increase and the threat of deportation. Overcrowding in the tenements, built next to the wharves for these labourers continued and was to cause innumerable difficulties.

The second decade of this century will long be remembered in Rangoon for the periodic outbreaks of the virulent diseases of the day, such as plague, cholera, and typhoid. Invariably, the chief victims were the lower classes who were forced to live in insanitary conditions. The influenza pan-epidemic of 1918-19 in particular, took a terrible toll and thousands died. Infant mortality was high; between 1919 and 1925, the death rate was over 350 per 1000.

In 1919, although India was to see extensive changes in the way it was governed, Burma was excluded from such reforms. This state of affairs was to cause further resentment among the Burmese, who were becoming more assertive and vociferous, much to the annoyance of the British. The feeling in Rangoon's mercantile and government circles was that the Burmese were no doubt very charming but totally incompetent. It was claimed that they did not even make good servants. One Pegu Club member was heard to declare "rotten servants, these Burmese! If you give them hell about something or other they'll leave you as soon as dammit; throw up their job Sir! Never have that sort of thing with Indians; pay 'em well, and you can curse the guts out of them. I mean to say, you know where you are with Indians".

Although the people's representative from among the non-Europeans was officially given certain powers in 1919, yet his role in Government was only in an advisory capacity, and did not carry weight. The two Ministers of the Transferred Side, who were representatives of the legislature, were allowed to make proposals, yet, unless the Governor, advised by two of his Members of Council for the Reserve Side agreed, the proposals could not be passed into law.

In 1919, the Wunthanu Association was formed which encouraged the boycotting of British goods. This turned out to be a great success, and was taken up all over the country, although it was noticed that there were excitable young rogues and monks with small canes doing the rounds of the bazaars, thrashing offenders and enforcing the boycott. The first to experience the effects of these drastic measures were the British merchants in Rangoon who complained bitterly, but were powerless to do anything about it.

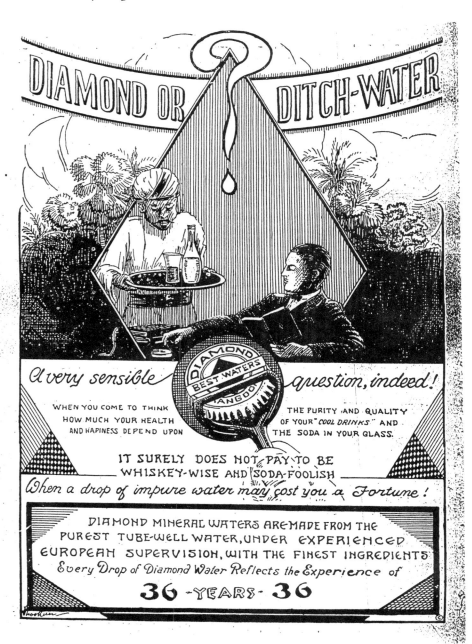

ပြည်တွင်းရေကြောင်းပို့ဆောင်ရေး
INLAND WATER TRANSPORT

ဂျမ်ခါနာအသင်း ဝင်များ ၏ ဇာတ်သိမ်း

Last Orders at the Gymnkhana

END OF AN ERA
1920-1942

With the end of the First World War, trade in Rangoon began to pick up, and within a short space of time the price of rice rose sharply. However, much to the undisguised disappointment of the British who traded in this commodity, the Burma Government prevented them from selling at the world price, as it would have had a detrimental effect on the farmers of the country. The Government then bought the Burma rice at a fixed rate, and resold it on the outside market at the current price. It was proposed that part of the profits be used in funding projects for making improvements in public works and education in the country.

Among the Burmese upper classes and civil servants of Rangoon, it had now become the accepted practice to provide their sons with the very best education. Many attended the University of Calcutta, while the more fortunate were sent to London. The ambition of these students was to secure of a post in one of the government departments. This was despite the existence of a situation whereby although an Englishman and a Burman performed similar duties, there was a vast difference in their salaries. Certain privileges were also denied to the latter. As nothing could be done to improve conditions, it had to be accepted by all applicants for the time being.

However, attitudes were already changing among the young Burmese, and on December 20 1920, the newly established University of Rangoon witnessed the first strike by its students. The walk out had been provoked by the University of Rangoon Act which made sure that the council members and administrators were all government nominees and British; this was blatantly anti-Burmese. So strong were the national feelings against the government that the strike soon spread to other schools.

Above: Carved wooden door and window, China Town.
Left: Detail of the former Irrawaddy Flotilla Company building on Phayre (Pansodan) Street.

187

Rangoon Railway Station
(usually referred to as
Phayre Street Station).
c.1910.

ရန်ကုန်ဘူတာကြီး

The authorities responded by publishing the names of students to be expelled, at the same time threatening the parents who were in the civil service that their employment would be terminated unless they agreed to make their sons call off the strike. Fortunately, Government finally cancelled both threats, and the students returned to their studies after suitable amendments had been made to the Act.

In January 1922, the city played host to the youthful Edward, the Prince of Wales, on his gruelling but successful Eastern Tour, during which he was made welcome by the numerous subjects of the Empire. Fawningly worded banners, such as 'Tell Daddy We Are All Happy Under British Rule', lined the official routes in several of the countries. In Rangoon, the usual routine was followed, and dancing girls and elaborate tinsel triumphal arches were everywhere. Although agitators were lurking in the streets, the police saw to it that they were kept well in the background.

The city was again in a holiday mood. There was the Proclamation Parade and the pony races at which the Prince's Cup was presented to a delighted Chinese. At a huge garden party at Government House, the Prince wearing his solar topee sat surrounded by richly dressed Burmese matrons, while an elegant and bejewelled maiden who was seated next to him explained the meaning of the Burmese classical dance; Rangoon's malicious gossips later made unfounded claims that the poor girl was carrying his child.

The 'fabled' city of Mandalay was visited next, where the Prince played polo, and was entertained by the Shan Chiefs in their 'gorgeously grotesque robes'; numerous tribal dances were performed and viewed by the visitors with polite interest. The author's mother remembers coyly singing a silly little song together with other schoolgirls as the Prince drove by:

Oh we love you Prince of Wales
More than we can say
Do you live far away,
Far from Mandalay?

Back in Rangoon, a splendid regatta was held on the Royal Lakes, on which the Prince and his suite were rowed for some time in a gleaming state-barge. At night the whole area was lit with 'prismatic fairy lamps and thousands of Chinese lanterns, and a procession of illuminated boats,

...no more romantic page in the annals of the development of the Empire can be found than the history of the growth of this small town of thatched huts, which passed under British occupation in 1852, into this vast metropolis and prosperous port of today...Here railways and craft of the two great river valleys of Burma deliver up spoils of your mines, your oil-fields, your rice plantations, and your forests to the factories and docks of this city. The shipping of all lands seeks your port to carry your produce to the four corners of the world...Your city is in a true sense the capital of Burma, for in your midst stands the great pagoda, the oldest of all holy places of religion, claiming a large proportion of followers among the human race than any other, and this building is a supreme expression of the genius of the Burmese people.

EDWARD, PRINCE OF WALES, AT THE LEWIS STREET JETTY, 1922.

Aerial photograph of the Secretariat (now called *Wungyi-mya-yon*) taken in the 1930s. ရန်ကုန်မြို့ ဝန်ကြီးများ ရဲ

led by the Royal Barge, wound in and out of the little bays, while the sky blazed with fireworks'. Edward watched all this from Scandal Point. Mrs Simpson and the crisis of his future abdication were still a long way off. As the Prince's vessel steamed out of the Rangoon Harbour, voices from a nearby launch rose in song 'Will ye no' come back again?'

In 1923, Burma was granted dyarchy (dual government) which was now in force in India, but this was to prove unworkable, the main problem being that control was still in the hands of the India Government. It also caused considerable friction between the various Burmese political parties, which were mainly based in Rangoon. To add to the problem, personality clashes soon occurred among the Burmese ministers who were elected to office.

During this period, when some of the more senior Shan Sawbwas (Chiefs) paid the Lieutenant-Governor an official visit either in Rangoon or at Maymyo, they were entitled to a salute of nine guns. Yet attitudes were such that it would have been unthinkable to invite these nobles to dinner at Government House. Membership of the three premier clubs in the city were also denied not only to these men, but also to the highest ranking Burmese civil servants. A request by those who were foolhardy enough to apply would certainly have been rejected. Until well into the 1930s, it was firmly believed by many of the British administrators that the only way to maintain respect from the Burmese was to treat them as underlings.

The Pegu Club was still the stronghold of the senior civil service, while the Gymkhana and the Boat Clubs continued to be patronized by the mercantile community. Perhaps, with the upsurge of nationalistic feelings among the Burmese, there was a tightening of attitudes by the British who felt that their lifestyle was being threatened. Many believed that a last stand had to be made by opposing the relaxing of the rigid social barriers which they had successfully erected around themselves. At this time, emotions were running so high that the very thought of allowing non-Europeans to enter the exclusive interiors of their clubs were genuinely distressing to many.

British merchants also felt that as they had dealings with Indian businessman, whom they considered to be socially inferior, the idea of meeting them on equal terms was out of the question. And as far as the Burmese were concerned, since they had very little part to play in the foreign commerce of the city, most Britishers were unaware of them, so that business communication with them was rarely established. Many an Englishman lived in Burma for years without ever speaking a word of the language or possessing the slightest awareness of the country's history, and never for a moment entertaining the faintest idea about the people's religious beliefs.

As discussed above, for Englishmen who were rash enough to take a Burmese wife, life outside the family home could be made uncomfortable by the *sahibs* and their *memsahibs*. The native wife could not be invited into the home of an Englishwoman, let alone take tea at the Gymkhana Club. Under these circumstances, the men had no choice but to cut themselves off socially from the British community, sometimes forming little groups with others in similar situations. Yet on grand occasions, the great lawn at Government House swarmed with a multitude of races.

When Sir Reginald Craddock, the Lieutenant-Governor, was introduced to the historian Gordon Luce, he accused him of being pro-Burman. This was almost an insult, implying that he was being treacherous to his own race. Luce was a great scholar who was later to become celebrated for his researches into Burmese history and archaeology, but at the time had committed the unforgivable crime of marrying a Burmese woman.

By 1922, the Municipal Corporation of the City of Rangoon was administered by thirty-four

Councillors, of these, twenty-nine were elected and the remainder nominated by the Local Government. Also elected were ten Burmese; five Europeans; four each from among the Hindus and Muslims; two Chinese; and one representative each from the Development Trust, Trades Association, Chamber of Commerce, and the Port Commissioners.

With an economic revival, many of the older buildings in the commercial sector were demolished, to be replaced by massive and grander structures. Pulled down, too, were some of the earlier wooden houses which were originally intended to be occupied by a single family. Some of these had been lovingly built with carved verandahs, ornamental windows, and roof decorations. As space was now at a premium, multi-storied masonry blocks containing tiny flats took their place. Earlier in 1913 Dautrimer had predicted that once the old wooden buildings had been pulled down parts of Rangoon would look like any other town in Europe or England.

The removal in 1926 of the military from its Cantonment near Pagoda Hill, and of the Rangoon Turf Club by the Jubilee Hall, meant that large areas of much needed land were finally transferred to the Municipality. As a result of which the expansion northwards now escalated. This was spearheaded at Kamayut by the creation of a new and sprawling University of Rangoon estate, bordering on the magnificent Kokine Lakes (now Inya Lakes).

In that year also, after a thorough overhaul of the vast network of roads, the electric trams and the bus services were revived. The building of new roads also meant that the long awaited development of the suburbs to the north could now be stepped up. To the west, the sewage contaminated areas near Lanmadaw were covered over, and the level raised. On completion, housing sites were properly laid out with drains, streets, and other public amenities. Despite these improvements and the increase in habitation areas, there was still a housing shortage as the poorer classes from the regions continued to pour into Rangoon to take up residence.

Somerset Maugham, who visited Rangoon in the late 1920s, felt that there was nothing distinctive about the city, and said that he could have been driving through either Alexandria or Shanghai. On the other hand, he was much taken by the towering Shwedagon with its profusion of small shrines and pavilions which clustered around it.

As trade continued to improve, the Rangoon docks with their huge hydraulic cranes, were illuminated at night by electricity so that round the clock shifts were possible during busy periods. The new prosperity resulted in a further influx of coolies from the Indian subcontinent. As all the available land near the river front had been bought up by the mercantile firms to build offices, much needed extra accommodation for the labourers could not proceed. Overcrowding in the notorious lodging-houses for the labourers continued, and in 1925 alone the number of prosecutions against the landlords rose to 1,414. These grasping villains of the day blatantly ignored the altruistic protests of the Social Service League.

Among the younger members of the British community, social attitudes were gradually changing, and by the end of the Twenties, clubs in the smaller towns were already permitting leading non-Europeans to join as honorary members, and including them in all the social activities.

In Rangoon, many of the once rural areas north of the Shwedagon were now becoming much sought after. The remaining pockets of tiny mat and bamboo hamlets which blocked the path of this expansion northward were finally removed, and in their place substantial and impressive residences with large gardens began to be built. Churchill Road, and the appropriately named Golden Valley, with its rural atmosphere, were to become for a time an enclave of the British

Advert for the Burmah Oil Company. *The Rangoon Times*, 1936.

၁၉၃၆ခုနှစ်မှ ပန် ချိဆရာကြီ ဦ ဘဏ္ဍဏ်၏လက်ရာ

Advert for the Burmah Oil Company with a painting by Ba Nyan, the first Burmese artist to study in London and hold an exhibition at Government House. *The Rangoon Times* (Christmas Number) 1937.

၁၉၃၇ခုနှစ်မှ ပန်ချီဆရာကြီ ဦးဘဉာဏ်၏လက်ရာ

A cartoon on the reluctance of Europeans to remove their shoes within pagoda precincts. It pokes fun at some of the sycophantic Burmese of the time. *Thuriya* (Sun) a Burmese language magazine, 1918.

မျက်နှာလုပ်လိုသူများ၊ ၁၉၁၈ခုနှစ်မှ ကာတွန်းဆရာ ဦးဘကလေး၏ လက်ရာ

elite. But much to their irritation, as properties became vacant the houses were bought by wealthy Burmese and Indian families.

For the British boating set the Rangoon Sailing Club on the Kokine Lakes now provided an additional place of recreation. It was strictly 'Europeans Only' and was claimed to be even more exclusive than the other three venerable clubs.

For some time now, usually at the beginning of each cool season, Rangoon had been visited by what was known as the 'fishing fleet'. These were young, and more often not so young single ladies from England who came out to stay with a relative. Such new arrivals had matrimony in mind and tended to 'come out' at the Gymkhana. Fortunately for many they were unaware of the epithet by which they were known to the local British male population. 'Off to the Gymkhana to review the Fishing Fleet', became the standard remark of the bachelors in the city. Sadly, there was no guarantee that any one of these hopefuls would land a 'catch'. Charles Allen, in his book on the Raj, said that the term was first coined in the early part of the nineteenth century when groups of Englishwomen bravely went out to India in search of husbands; the unsuccessful ones who gave up and went home were cruelly referred to as 'Returned Empties'.

Others who were more fortunate found husbands, usually well established older men from among the civil service, mercantile or military communities. As a *burra-memsahib*, such a person was carefully 'groomed' by other great ladies, and rapidly acquired the talent for organising 'delightful little dinner-parties', and having the knack of making sure that her guests, especially those who were lower down in the pecking order, knew their place - it was all done so charmingly.

In May of 1930, Rangoon society was present at a lavish garden party given by Sir Po Tha, a Burmese landowner of immense wealth. 800 guests, consisting of Europeans and non-Europeans were invited, and on arrival, an envelope containing a gold sovereign was handed to each. Although the party was a great success, many of the English ladies complained that the gift was a trifle vulgar - but accepted it nevertheless. The complacency, however, of this little world was soon to be shattered.

Burma, the Land of Sunshine and Gilded Temples was not destined to escape the economic depression which had descended on the rest of the world. Rice prices fell alarmingly, and in the countryside thousands of Burmese farmers who had no savings lost their lands and homes to the despised Chetty-kala (Indian moneylenders). Rumours spread that it was a plot by the British to help the Indian immigrants and hatred towards this industrious community began to build up again.

With the predictable increase in unemployment, resentment was felt by Burmese labourers at the foreign coolies who were prepared to work for lower wages, and who now dominated the labour market in Rangoon and elsewhere. There were now more than one million Indians living in Burma, the largest number of any country in South East Asia. The mercantile classes among them had spread out over the country and were firmly established in all the larger towns. Some of the younger Indians further irritated the Burmese by boasting that they were soon to make a commercial conquest of all Asia.

On May 5 1930, Mahatma Gandhi was arrested in India, and on the same day a violent earthquake struck Rangoon. Although the epicentre was near Pegu, which suffered appalling destruction, there was also damage to property within the capital, with many killed. Some of the Indians in the city were so emotionally overcome by the two events, which they were convinced were connected, that they ran through the streets stoning passers by.

At the docks, the Indian coolies decided to go on strike, which left the port authorities no alternative but to hire Burmese labour. But unknown to the Burmese and those who hired them, the strike had ended as suddenly as it had begun. When the Burmese turned up for work the following day, they were abruptly informed that their services were no longer required. Their anger was further inflamed when the crowds of Indians who were now returning to work laughed at them. The Burmese are notoriously quick-tempered and in an instant there was a riot. As the furious Burmese attacked, their opponents naturally fought back, but many were thrown into the swift flowing river, or were hacked to death. Other Indians were quick to seek reprisal. As news spread that a young Burmese girl had had her breasts sliced off, hundreds of armed men from the Burmese quarters poured into the city in the direction of the Indian sector. Fortunately, a group of British officers who could speak Burmese arrived, and finally persuaded some of these irate bands to give up their arms and disperse.

Jubilee Hall (1898). Built to commemorate Queen Victoria's Diamond Jubilee it was the place where Rangoons society gathered. It has since been demolished.

ရန်ကုန်မြို့၏ ကျက်သရေဆောင် ဂျူဘလီခမ်းမဆောင်

Phayre Street, since renamed Pansodan Street. In the main photo the central building is the Inland Water Transport Board and was formerly the offices of the Irrawaddy Flotilla Co. The building above is the National Museum, which before Independence was Grindlay's bank, and below is the Port Authority building.

MSS Eur D1230/9

ORIGINAL PAINTING BY   BA NYAN.

THE
RANGOON
CORPORATION

BANQUET

JUBILEE HALL
THE 5TH DECEMBER 1930

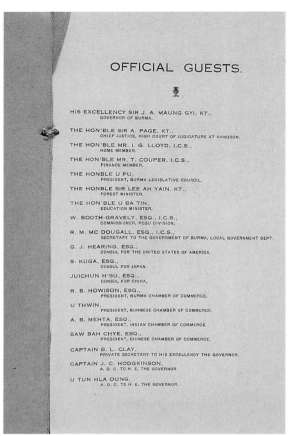

OFFICIAL GUESTS.

HIS EXCELLENCY SIR J. A. MAUNG GYI, KT.,
GOVERNOR OF BURMA.

THE HON'BLE SIR A. PAGE, KT.,
CHIEF JUSTICE, HIGH COURT OF JUDICATURE AT RANGOON.

THE HON'BLE MR. I. G. LLOYD, I.C.S.,
HOME MEMBER.

THE HON'BLE MR. T. COUPER, I.C.S.,
FINANCE MEMBER.

THE HONBLE U PU,
PRESIDENT, BURMA LEGISLATIVE COUNCIL.

THE HONBLE SIR LEE AH YAIN, KT.,
FOREST MINISTER.

THE HON'BLE U BA TIN,
EDUCATION MINISTER,

W. BOOTH-GRAVELY, ESQ., I.C.S.,
COMMISSIONER, PEGU DIVISION.

R. M. MC DOUGALL, ESQ., I.C.S.,
SECRETARY TO THE GOVERNMENT OF BURMA, LOCAL GOVERNMENT DEPT.

G. J. HEARING, ESQ.,
CONSUL FOR THE UNITED STATES OF AMERICA.

S. KUGA, ESQ.,
CONSUL FOR JAPAN.

JUICHUN H'SU, ESQ.,
CONSUL FOR CHINA.

R. B. HOWISON, ESQ.,
PRESIDENT, BURMA CHAMBER OF COMMERCE.

U THWIN,
PRESIDENT, BURMESE CHAMBER OF COMMERCE.

A. B. MEHTA, ESQ.,
PRESIDENT, INDIAN CHAMBER OF COMMERCE.

SAW BAH CHYE, ESQ.,
PRESIDENT, CHINESE CHAMBER OF COMMERCE.

CAPTAIN B. L. CLAY,
PRIVATE SECRETARY TO HIS EXCELLENCY THE GOVERNOR.

CAPTAIN J. C. HODGKINSON,
A. D. C. TO H. E. THE GOVERNOR.

U TUN HLA OUNG,
A. D. C. TO H. E. THE GOVERNOR.

As a police cordon was placed around the Indian quarter, many of its men began arming themselves, ready to fight. Understandably, panic stricken Rangoon was brought to a standstill. Hundreds of essential workers in the Indian community went into hiding to avoid the ferocity of the Burmese attacks. Their terrified families rushed to take refuge in the grounds of the old Rangoon Lunatic Asylum, which was now standing empty as new premises had been built elsewhere. In a building which was originally designed to take five hundred patients, there were now over 7,000 low caste Indians, many of them with hideous wounds, and without food. To add to the problems, the collection of night-soil came to an abrupt end, as this was performed only by this group.

It was claimed that during the four days of rioting, between 300 and 500 Indians were killed, and hundreds more wounded, but no one was brought to trial and no compensation paid to the victims. The Burmese elite were appalled by the massacres, and felt that it had happened at an inopportune moment when they were trying to let London know that they were capable, and ready for a constitutional government.

But the city was to witness another incident on June 24, when the 1,100 or so convicts in the Rangoon Jail mutinied. The cause of the mutiny was the illtreatment inflicted by the Indian Superintendent on the Burmese convicts. During what amounted to a reprisal, the Military Police, made up of Indians, set up a continuous fire from their positions on the walls on many of the unarmed inmates; thirty-four Burmans were killed in this attack.

On the very day of the mutiny, a report by the Simon Commission was published, which contained the proposal for the separation of Burma from India; something the Burmese nationalists had been fighting for. To many among the British and European population all these incidents were merely an irritation, as they continued with their social whirl.

In August 1930, when Sir Charles Innes, the Governor, departed on sick leave, Sir Joseph Maung Gyi became the first Burmese to be appointed acting-governor. Despite his exalted position he was still denied access to the great clubs. At the time, Ba Nyan, one of the first Burmese artists to train in London, was in Rangoon, and Maurice Collis persuaded Sir Joseph to hold an exhibition at Government House. This was the first exhibition of its kind to which the city's multi cultural society was invited - including the Japanese consular representative, who remained unrecognised socially by the English community. It was later said that the idea of a Burmese artist exhibiting in the hallowed halls of Government House was all too much for some senior members of the civil service, and Sir Joseph was privately rebuked.

On October 28 1930, the authorities were suddenly made aware of the fact that a mysterious character who called himself Saya San, had declared himself king of Burma, with the title of Thupannaka Galon Raja or King of the Garuda Birds - a powerful and terrifying symbol among the Burmese. The man was a renegade priest, who dabbled in astrology and magic, believing that he had the power to drive the British out of the country with spells. Seduced by his propaganda machine, thousands of gullible Burmese peasants flocked to his banner.

The coronation rites were held within the sacred grounds of the Myasein Taungyo Pagoda [Pagoda of the Emerald-green Mountain], about thirty minutes drive from central Rangoon. While the Burmese politicians realized that their goals could only be achieved by going to London and presenting their case, the naive and uneducated were all for attacking and destroying the British. The fact that it would have been an unequal battle did not appear to have deterred

" Come you back to Mandalay,
" Where the old Flotilla lay ;
" Can't you 'ear their paddles chunkin' from

Rangoon to Mandalay :

" On the road to Mandalay,
" Where the flyin' fishes play,
" An' the dawn comes up like thunder outer China 'crost the Bay !

What caused KIPLING to burst into Song will surely give you a Thrill of Pleasure.

The IRRAWADDY is just as Fascinating now as it was then and the best and most comfortable way to see it, is by STEAMER.

THE STEAMERS PROVIDE FOOD, BED AND BEDDING AND A REAL RESTFUL HOLIDAY.

IRRAWADDY FLOTILLA CO., LTD.
50, PHAYRE STREET, RANGOON.

WHEN TIME MEANS MONEY AND SPEED IS ESSENTIAL

TRAVEL BY AIR
REGULAR SERVICES OPERATED
WITH FOUR-ENGINED SEAPLANES, COMFORTABLE AND SAFE.
SEAPLANES FOR HIRE AT MODERATE RATES.

IRRAWADDY FLOTILLA & AIRWAYS Limited.
50, PHAYRE STREET

TELEPHONE NO. 7. **RANGOON.** TELEGRAMS "FLOTILLA."

Commercial building on
Strand Road. 1930s.

these simple country folk. Soon there was unrest in the country, as groups of armed thugs pretending to be followers of the new king began making their presence felt.

When the rebellion was finally crushed in 1932, it was claimed that 10,000 people had lost their lives. Sadly, many of the victims were poor farmers who had implicit faith in the supposed magical powers of the various leaders who now appeared. The three prominent men who masterminded the attacks were the magician-priest Bandaka, Saya Nyan, and the self proclaimed king Saya San. They were all hanged with their henchmen, but in the countryside the unsettled conditions were to continue.

Resentment of foreigners among some Burmese was such that during 1931 another riot occurred, but this time it was the Chinese who suffered. Unlike the more passive Indians, the Chinese, much to the surprise of their attackers, fought back. Again, lives and property were lost.

In that year, Burma was offered a constitution similar to that of India, but as agreement could not be reached between both parties the discussions dragged on. The intervening years were to witness many demonstrations in the streets of Rangoon, and the founding of new political parties among the younger men, who, unlike their elders were fast losing their awe of the European. These young men found the exclusive 'whites only' clubs particularly unpalatable, and resented the superior attitudes of the ruling race.

In central Rangoon there was much activity on the site of the old Ripon Hall, as the building of a new Town Hall had been resumed in the late 1920s. The authorities insisted that the structure should contain elements of Burmese architecture; this was to cause further delay in its construction. Finally, in 1936, the new Town Hall was completed and formally opened with grand ceremony by Sir Archibald Cochran, the Governor, who arrived in a carriage shaded by gold umbrellas.

Rangoon now had a building which was impressively Burmese, with all the traditional motifs of peacocks, lotus flowers and *naga* (dragons). The interior was equally splendid, with a grand sweeping staircase. Each doorway in the main hall was framed by intricately carved tapering ornaments in the royal style.

For many Burmese politicians, April 1 1937, brought the long awaited moment when Burma was finally separated from India. The country now enjoyed a full parliamentary government. Although there was a prime minister and a cabinet in Rangoon, they were given control only of the areas occupied by the Burmese race. Regions such as the Shan States, Chin and Kachin Hills to the north, together with defence and external affairs were still firmly held in the hands of the British Governor. Understandably, this was not to the liking of the political parties who insisted on complete control of the entire country.

It was claimed by the British that although everyone was talking about Burmese nationalism and self government, no one was quite sure what it was they wanted. Nevertheless they felt that they had to have it come what may. Among the Burmese, many believed that such a move was necessary if they were to check the problem of Indian immigration. Unfortunately, instead of consolidating their powers and working for the betterment of the country, the political parties and the ministers became obsessed with their own petty jealousies and devoted their energies to squabbling amongst themselves.

Examples of iron work found in the Downtown area of Rangoon.

Private residence on Halpin Road, now called Pyidaungsu Road. This house is now the Thai embassy.

In the late Thirties, the streets of Rangoon began experiencing traffic problems, with an assortment of smart motor cars, slow-moving bullock carts, *gharries*, and rickshaws jostling for space. Buses which had the pictures of animals painted in front, instead of the route numbers, weaved through the congestion. Sadly, many of the splendid Victorian buildings, such as the Post Office with its facade of wrought iron filigree had been demolished, to be replaced by huge functional structures of red brick.

In 1938, Rangoon was visited by Major Raven-Hart, whose ambition was to travel down the Irrawaddy River from Myitkyina, in the north, in his collapsible canoe. He was a marvellous character, with a refreshing attitude which was the very opposite of many of the stuffy colonials in the city. His book, *Canoe to Mandalay*, offers revealing insights into the life of the city of this period.

Raven-Hart recommended that the Pegu Club, which he likened to a 'Palaeontological Gallery', was worth visiting, 'just to see what used to be alive', referring to the old colonials, adding that here the 'fossils of Burma' could be studied. Travelling around the city, his observant eyes often picked out amusing sign boards in the Indian quarter, such as 'Remarkable and Clever in circumcising Moslem Children' and 'Very nice Cure for Leprosy'. He was warned by fellow Englishmen that as a white man he was not to use a rickshaw, as it just 'wasn't done'. Raven-Hart was amused to learn that newly arrived juniors in British firms had been severely told off by the

Above: Fancy dress party for European children in the grounds of private residence.

Below: Burmese schoolgirls. The little girls all have their hair dressed in the traditional *san-yit-waing* (circular hair fringe) style. c.late 1930s.

တို့ရင် ဆိတ်ရင်
ဗျာမျာ နေကြသော

head of department for this offence and promptly thought that it would be marvellous fun to turn up at the Pegu Club in one.

Raven-Hart also advised tourists that after days of 'Indian-ridden Rangoon' a visit to Kemmindine would reveal that there were Burmans in Burma. Perhaps he did not know that many had already settled in the eastern sector of the city. Since the 1880s, Rangoon had begun attracting from all over the country Burmese writers, craftsmen, and people from the world of the performing arts. Sustained by the wealth of the city each group had flourished in these quarters.

The Burmese film industry was founded in Rangoon as early as 1918, and there were now several companies producing a large number of films. In the area around the Sule Pagoda Road, there were several cinemas where Burmese films, together with imports from Europe, Hollywood, and India, could be seen. Despite the fondness of the Burmese public for traditional theatrical shows, the new film stars successfully competed with leading theatrical personalities like the celebrated actor-dancer Po Sein.

Nightlife for the Europeans continued as before, with many of the younger residents and tourists frequenting the new clubs and night spots in central Rangoon. As these establishments were more relaxed in their attitudes, they were not patronized by the older members of the British community. Nevertheless, at some, standards were maintained, and at the Silver Grill, gentlemen who wished to enjoy the delights within, had to wear a dinner-jacket to gain admittance. Here, cabaret acts from Europe and India were often featured.

Lower down the scale there were other clubs, such as the disreputable Montparnasse, a favourite haunt of sailors, where drunken fights were frequent. China Town, too, had its attractions, in particular its famous restaurants with their discreet upstairs dining cubicles. Here, each male guest was pampered by a young lady, who gave the impression that the sole aim in her life was to make his evening enjoyable.

Despite all this superficial gaiety, racial tensions between the various communities were never far away. In July 1938 anti-Muslim feelings suddenly erupted among the Burmese, resulting in outbreaks of violence and spasmodic fighting in Rangoon and other towns which was to last until February 1939. The trouble had begun when *Thuriya,* a Burmese language newspaper in Rangoon, published extracts from a book which included insulting comments about the Buddhist faith. As the author was a Muslim, the Islamic associations in Burma immediately disassociated themselves from the book and apologised. But the newspapers continued to stir up trouble and inflame racial hatred, resulting in riots in which over 200 Muslims were killed and hundreds more wounded. The looting and damage to property of the rich Muslim merchants was said to have been very high. Curiously, as in the earlier riots of 1930, neither arrests nor compensations were made.

During the riots of 1930, the British Governor had been responsible for security, but in 1939, this difficult task was now entirely in the hands of the Burmese Ministers. It was later discovered that the incident had been a politically motivated act, contrived by the opponents of the Prime Minister Dr Ba Maw; their aim which was to discredit him succeeded. This revelation was to cause many Europeans and Burmese in the police force to resign in protest.

But these were temporary setbacks, for trade figures showed that Rangoon was once again flourishing as a thriving commercial centre. From its docks, over 3,000,000 tons of rice a year were exported, more than half that of Thailand. Like the ancient Chinese port of Hang-chou, the city could, for a time, be called the 'Pearl of the Orient' - a title which was soon to be shattered by the onset of the Second World War, resulting in the destructive occupation of the country by the Imperial Armies of Japan.

As war descended on Europe, Rangoon was rife with rumours that the Burmese political parties were preparing for an open rebellion against the British. When intelligence was received that many of the leaders of these groups had been collecting private armies, orders were given by the Governor for their arrest. Others secretly contacted Japanese agents, who encouraged them to turn against the British, assuring them that they would help Burma gain independence. Though the country buzzed with talk of the coming war, a large majority of the population felt that Burma would not become involved. Such complacency, however, was shattered on December 23 1941, when Rangoon suffered its first air raid. Over eighty Japanese planes bombed the city, killing more than 2,000 people, while many of the panic-stricken survivors fled into the country-side. The bombing resumed on Christmas Day, when fifty-two enemy fighters were shot down by the Royal Air Force and the American Volunteer Group.

This second raid triggered another exodus from the stricken city and its environs. The refugees were mainly Indians who began streaming out of Rangoon in the direction of India, forced on by the collective fear that during the chaos which was bound to follow, they would be massacred by the Burmese. Before them lay the formidable barriers of Arakan and Manipur, where thousands were to perish of starvation and disease.

On January 19 1942, the Japanese landed at Tavoy and the invasion of Burma had begun. In Rangoon, the 'E' (evacuation) signal went up on February 20, and the plight of frightened people trying to escape intensified, leaving the city to raging fires and looters. With the exception of the demolition teams who were responsibile for the destruction of key installations, all other British personnel in Rangoon were ordered to leave.

The great city lay in ruins, its rubble-strewn streets now almost devoid of human beings. Many of the imposing buildings had been destroyed by the bombs and the resulting fires burned on unchecked. To add to the horror, a new terror was about to descend on the city.

It was discovered that the staff of the jails and lunatic asylums had left in a hurry, abandoning the thousands of inmates who were still locked in their cells. Fielding Hall, a young Under-Secretary in the Home Department, and son of the famous author, was informed of this, and becoming alarmed at the news that the Japanese were approaching the city, gave the order to release the inmates. By the time it was realized that this piece of intelligence was a false alarm, it was too late as hardened criminals, psychopaths, and crazed lunatics roamed the deserted streets of the city. They were joined by marauders, who smashed their way into houses and looted their contents. Among the citizens, those who would not, or could not bring themselves to leave their homes, barricaded themselves in, nerves stretched to breaking point. But they were defenceless against the armed and vicious thugs who now prowled the streets. Law and order had broken down completely and for over two weeks the city was given up to destruction, murder and rape. Although there was a small police and military presence, the men were powerless to intervene. As there were no longer any facilities to remove the numerous corpses, the bodies were burnt in the streets. Fielding Hall was so overcome at the thought of the horrors he had unleashed that he committed suicide.

For many of the Indians refugees other terrors awaited them when they were intercepted up country by the pro-Japanese Burmese guerillas. Evacuees were considered fair game and were robbed of their valuables, and ill treated, tales of rape and murder were common.

On March 7 1942, at two o'clock in the afternoon, selected Government buildings, important industrial installations, and anything which would be of use to the enemy were blown up by the demolition teams. Amongst these were the huge oil refineries at Syriam. Contemporary photographs show Rangoon engulfed by a thick pall of billowing black smoke and flames.

Above and behind this terrible screen of blazing fires, the miraculously unscathed golden cone of the Shwedagon glistened, detached and aloof. From its vantage point, it had been a witness to many atrocities in the past, and man's inhumanity to his fellow man was nothing new. Three long and brutal years were to pass before the City of the Pagoda and the rest of the country could be liberated from the Japanese. But by then, the Gymkhana, that great bastion of the Raj, was already a pile of smouldering rubble.

SELECT BIBLIOGRAPHY

Alexander, J. E., *Travels from India to England; Comprehending a Journey through Persia, Asia Minor, European Turkey, etc., in the Year 1825-26,* Parbury, Allen & Co., London, 1827.

Allen, Charles, *Raj: A Scrapbook of British India, 1877-1947,* Andre Deutsch Ltd., 1977, reprinted Penguin Books Ltd., Harmondsworth, Middlesex, 1979.

Baird, J. G. A., (ed) *Private Letters of the Marquess of Dalhousie,* William Blackwood & Sons, Edinburgh, 1910.

Ballhatchet, Kenneth, *Race, Sex and Class Under the Raj,* Weidenfeld & Nicholson Ltd., London, 1990.

Blagden, C. O.,'Mon Inscriptions; Section II, The Medieval Mon Records, No.XII, The Inscriptions of the Kalyanisima, Pegu', *Epigraphia Birmanica,* Government Printing & Stationery, Burma, 1934.

'An Inscription on the Shwedagon Pagoda', *Epigraphia Birmanica,* vol. IV, Part I, Government Printing & Stationery, Rangoon, 1934.

British Burma Gazetteer, Government Press, Rangoon, 1880.

Chen Yi Sein, 'The Chinese in Rangoon During the 18th and 19th Centuries', *Essays Offered to Luce,* Artibus Asiae, vol.II, Switzerland, 1966.

Collis, M., *Trials in Burma,* Faber and Faber Ltd., London, 1938.

The Grand Peregrination being the life and adventures of Fernao Mendes Pinto, Faber and Faber Ltd., London, 1949.

The Journey Outward, Faber and Faber Ltd., 1952.

Crawfurd, J., *Journal of an Embassy from the Governor-General of India to the Court of Ava, in the Year 1827,* Henry Colburn, London, 1829.

Dalrymple, A., *Oriental Repertory,* William Ballintine, London, 1808.

Dautrimer, Joseph, *Burma Under British Rule,* T. Fisher Unwin, London, 1913.

Del Mar, Walter, *The Romantic East: Burma, Assam, & Kashmir,* Adam & Charles Black, London, 1906.

Dufferin, Harriot Lady, *Our Viceregal Life in India: Selections from my Journal, 1884-1888,* John Murray, London, 1890.

Edmonds, Paul, *Peacocks and Pagodas,* George Routeledge & Sons, Ltd., London, 1924.

Fraser, W. G., 'Old Rangoon', *Journal of the Burma Research Society,* Rangoon, 1920.

Furnivall, J. S.,'Notes on the History of Hanthawaddy', pts. I-IV, *Journal of the Burma Research Society,* Rangoon, 1913-14.

'The History of Syriam', *Journal of the Burma Research Society,* Rangoon, 1915.

Fytche, Albert, *Burma Past and Present,* Kegan Paul, London, 1878.

Gerini, G. E., Col., *Researches on Ptolemy's Geography of Eastern Asia (Further India and Indo-Malay Archipelago),* Royal Asiatic Society, 22 Albermarle Street, London, 1909.

Glass, Leslie. *The Changing of Kings: Memories of Burma, 1934-1949.* Peter Owen, London 1985.

Gordon, C. A., *Our Trip to Burmah,* Balliere, Tindall & Cox, London, 1875.

Gouger, Henry, *Personal Narrative of Two Years' Imprisonment in Burmah,* John Murray, London, 1860.

Halliday, R., (ed)'Slapat rajawan datow smin ron' [The History of [Mon]Kings], *Journal of the Burma Research Society,* XIII, 1, Rangoon, 1923.

Hart, Mrs Ernest, *Picturesque Burma, Past and Present*, J. M. Dent & Co., London, 1897.

Harvey, G. E., *History of Burma: From the earliest Times to 10 March 1824, the Beginning of the English Conquest*, Longman, Green & Co., London,1925.

Hmawbee Saya Thein, 'Rangoon in 1852', *Journal of the Burma Research Society*, 2:2 (1912) p.185, Rangoon.

Htin Aung, Maung, *A History of Burma*, Columbia University Press, New York, 1967.

Kelly, R. T., *Burma Painted and Described*, Adam and Charles Black, London,1905.

Laurie, W. F. B., *Our Burmese Wars*, Allen, London, 1880.

Lloyd, Christopher, *Captain Marryat and the Old Navy*, Longmans, Green & Co., London, 1939.

Luce, Gordon H., *Old Burma-Early Pagan*, 3 vols. J. J. Augustin, Lotus Valley, New York, 1969-70.

McCrae, Alister, *Scots in Burma: Golden Times in a Golden Land*, Kiscadale Publications, 1990.

Marks, J. E., Dr., *Forty Years in Burma*, Hutchinson & Co., London, 1919.

Maybury, Maurice, *Heaven-Born in Burma: Flight of the Heaven-Born*, vol. 2, Folio Hadspen, Somerset, 1985.

Mitton, G. E., (Lady Scott), *Scott of the Shan Hills: Orders and Impressions*, John Murray, London, 1936.
    Bachelor Girl in Burma, Adam & Charles Black, London, 1907.

Montgomery Hyde, H., *The Cleveland Street Scandal*, W. H. Allen, London, 1976.

Nai Pan Hla, 'Mon Literature and Culture over Thailand and Burma', *Journal of the Burma Research Society*, 41:1 (1958), Rangoon.
    Yazadirit Ayedawpon Kyan - a biography of King Rajadarit (the Mon original was called *Rajadhiraj*), Min Hlaing Htaw Sarpay Press, Rangoon, 1977. [Burmese text].

O'Coonor, V.C. Scott, *Mandalay and Other Cities of the Past in Burma*, Hutchinson and Co., London, 1907.

Nisbet, John, *Burma Under British Rule - and Before*, 2 vols., Archibald Constable & Co Ltd., London, 1901.

Pearn, B. R., *A History of Rangoon*, American Baptist Mission Press, Rangoon, 1939.

Pe Maung Tin, 'The Shwe Dagon Pagoda', *Journal of the Burma Research Society*, vol.XXIV, no.1, Rangoon, 1934.

Pemberton, John, *A Collection of the Best and Most Interesting Voyages and Travels in all Parts of the World*, Longman, Hurst, Rees, Orme, and Brown, London, 1811.

Prevost Battersby, H.F. *India Under Royal Eyes,* George Allen, London 1906.

Rangoon (Sights and Institutions), Ministry of Union Culture, Rangoon, 1955.

Raven-Hart, R., Major, *Canoe to Mandalay*, The Book Club, London, 1939.

Reed, Stanley. *The Royal Tour in India*, Bennett, Coman & Co., Bombay, 1906.

Rhys Davids, T. W., *Buddhist Birth Stories*, The Pali Text Society, London, 1880.

Robertson, H. R., *A Modern De Quincy: An Autobiography*, George G. Harrap & Co., London, 1942.

Sangermano, Vincentius, *The Burmese Empire a Hundred Years Ago*, Archibald Constable & Co., London, 1893.

Shorto, H. L.,'The 32 Myos in the Medieval Mon Kingdom': *Bulletin of the School of Oriental and African Studies*, London University, London, 1963.
    'The Dewatau Sotapan: A Mon Prototype of the 37 Nats', *Bulletin of the School of Oriental and African Studies*, London University, London, 1967.

Shu Shin, Maung, *Myat-phaya Shwedagon* [The Sacred Shwedagon], Sarpaybeikman Press, Rangoon, 1972. [Burmese text].

Shwe Yoe (Sir George Scott), *The Burman, His Life and Notions*, Macmillan and Co., London, 1896; reprinted Kiscadale Publications, Edinburgh, 1989.

Shwe Zan Aung, Maung, 'Hypnotism in Burma', *Journal of the Burma Research Society,* 2:1 (1912), p.44, Rangoon.

Singer, Noel F., *Burmah: A Photographic Journey, 1855-1925,* Kiscadale Publications, Scotland, 1993.

'The Gold Relics of Bana Thau', *Arts of Asia,* September-October, 1992.

'Maha Bandula The Younger', *Arts of Asia,* November-December, 1994.

Stewart, A. T. Q., *The Pagoda War: Lord Dufferin and the fall of the Kingdom Ava, 1885-6,* Victorian (& Modern History) Book Club, Newton Abbot, 1974.

Stuart, John, *Burma Through the Centuries,* Kegan Paul, London, 1910.

Subindu, Thein, 'The testimony of an inhabitant of the city of Ava', *Journal of the Siam Society,* vol. 45 (2), Bangkok, 1957.

Swinhoe, Rodway, *The Incomplete Guide to Burma,* Rangoon Times Press, c.1923.

Sykes, W. H.,Col., 'Golden Relics at Rangoon', *Journal of the Royal Asiatic Society,* London, 1860.

Symes, Michael, *An Account of an Embassy to the Kingdom of Ava sent by the Governor-General of India in the Year 1795,* 3 vols., The Oriental Press, London, 1800.

Taw Sein Ko, *Burmese Sketches,* British Burma Press, 1913.

'A Preliminary Study of the Kalyani Inscriptions of Dhammacheti,1476 A.D.,' *The Indian Antiquary,* January, 1893, Kegan Paul, Trench, Trubner & Co., London.

Tennyson Jesse, F., *The Story of Burma,* Macmillian & Co. Ltd., London, 1946.

Tin Hla Thaw, 'A Historical Geography of Maritime Burma', *The Guardian,* December, 1966, Rangoon.

Tin, Mg Mg, U, *Konbaungset Mahayazawindawgyi* [Chronicle of the Konbaung Dynasty], 3 vols., Laitimantaing Press, Rangoon, 1967. [Burmese text].

Trant, T. A., *Two Years in Ava from May 1824 to May 1826, by an officer on the staff of the Quarter Master's Department,* John Murray, London, 1827.

Turley, Charles, *With the Prince Round the Empire,* Methuen & Co. Ltd., London, 1926.

Twinthintaik Wun Maha Sithu, *Twinthin Myanmar Yazawinthit* [Twinthin New Chronicle], Mingala Press, Rangoon, 1968, [Burmese text].

Warren, C. V., *Burmese Interlude,* Skeffington & Co Ltd., London, 1937.

White, Herbert Thirkell, Sir, *A Civil Servant in Burma,* Edward Arnold, London, 1913.

Also consulted were nineteenth century newspapers and magazines printed in British India and London, and Burmese language texts.

The Bengal Hurkaru
The Bombay Gazettee
The Englishman
The Madras Althenaeum
The Rangoon Gazettee
The Times of India
The Graphic
The Illustrated London News
The Mirror

INDEX